SOUVENIR PROGRAMME

IN SUPPORT OF THE RAF100 APPEAL

On this, the centenary of its formation, I send my heartfelt congratulations to the Royal Air Force at home and overseas, and to all of its families and loved ones.

The anniversary of the world's first independent Air Force is of great significance, and it is fitting to pay tribute to the tenacity, skill and sacrifice of the men and women who have served within its ranks over the last century, and who have defended our freedom so gallantly.

Through its enduring focus on professionalism, excellence and innovation, the Royal Air Force stands as a shining example of inspiration around the World today and for the next generations.

May the glory and honour that all ranks have bestowed on the Royal Air Force light its pathway to the future, guarding our skies and reaching for the stars.

Per Ardua ad Astra.

ELIZABETH R.

WELCOME

The 100th Anniversary of the formation of the Royal Air Force is an outstanding opportunity to commemorate, celebrate and inspire: to commemorate with pride 100 years of remarkable success, courage and sacrifice; to celebrate the achievements of today's RAF; and to inspire future generations to realise their ambitions and potential.

Our Centenary is not just about telling people what we do. It is also about letting everyone know who we are as an organisation – open to all, interested only in a person's merit, with a world-class reputation for training and development, always aiming for excellence.

The RAF is currently busier than we have been for at least a generation, from defending the skies of the UK, to fighting Da'esh in Iraq and Syria, from operations with NATO in Europe and in Afghanistan, to disaster relief in the Caribbean following Hurricane Irma. We have an outstanding record of responding quickly, successfully, and in force to emerging crises, deploying and sustaining aircraft and supporting capabilities at considerable range, in a way that can only be delivered by our air and space power.

The RAF100 Appeal is a vital part of our overall campaign and draws together our principal charities – the RAF Association, the RAF Benevolent Fund, the RAF Charitable Trust and the RAF Museum – in a wide range of national and regional fundraising events and activities, to ensure that we can both support the RAF100 aim of reaching out to future generations, while also looking after the needs of the whole RAF Family, serving and veteran.

The most important thing in RAF100 will be the legacy we leave beyond 2018 and into the RAF's second century. The foundations of that legacy already exist in the heritage and ethos of our first hundred years. It is a legacy built upon daily by our outstanding men and women as they demonstrate their excellence in air and space power. And it is a legacy we will secure for our second hundred years by using RAF100 to help inspire young people from across the nation.

Air Chief Marshal Sir Stephen Hillier
KCB CBE DFC ADC MA RAF

CONTENTS

Royal correspondence   8

A century of achievement   11

RAF timeline   14

A force for good   22

Full STEM ahead   27

Back to school   30

Passing on the centenary message   31

Women of the RAF   34

The challenge ahead   40

A display of air power   44

Forging inspiration   49

The RAF100 Flypast   50

    Flying in style   51

    Maintaining the force   55

    The Flypast sections   58

Acknowledgements   77

RAF100 Appeal sponsors   78

Credits   80

ROYAL CORRESPONDENCE

The name, formation and early achievements of the Royal Air Force are easy to take for granted, but as these letters and announcements from His Majesty King George V show, that was far from the case 100 years ago

TRUE COPY

(SIGNED) GEORGE R.I.

GEORGE THE FIFTH, by the Grace of God, of the United Kingdom of Great Britain and Ireland and of the British Dominions beyond the Seas. King, Defender of the Faith.

To all to whom these Presents shall come,

Greeting!

WHEREAS by the Air Force (Constitution) Act, 1917, it is enacted that it shall be lawful for Us to raise and maintain a Force, to be called the Air Force, consisting of such number of officers, warrant officers, non-commissioned officers and men as may from time to time be provided by Parliament:

NOW KNOW YE that it is our Will and Pleasure that the Air Force to be established pursuant to the said Act shall be styled the "Royal Air Force".

Given at the Court of Saint James's the 7th day of March, 1918

In the Eight Year of Our Reign.

By His Majesty's Command.

(Signed) Rothermere

Above

Much to the disappointment of the Air Council responsible for the formation of Britain's new independent air service, the name it was given in the Air Force (Constitution) Act of 1917 did not include the prefix "Royal". However, shortly before its formation on 1 April 1918, King George V graciously gave his consent to the name Royal Air Force for the new service.

Below

This telegram from King George V to the Secretary of State for the Royal Air Force, Lord Rothermere, was sent to congratulate him on the formation of the Royal Air Force on 1 April 1918. The rapid amalgamation of the two existing air services, the Royal Naval Air Service and the Royal Flying Corps, into a single independent Royal Air Force owed a great deal to Lord Rothermere's enthusiasm and drive during his brief period in office.

BUCKINGHAM PALACE

LORD ROTHERMERE. AIR MINISTRY. STRAND.

Today the Royal Air Force, of which you are Minister in Charge, comes into existence as a third arm of the Defences of the Empire.   As General-in-Chief I congratulate you on its birth, and I trust that it may enjoy a vigorous and successful life.

I am confident that the union of the Royal Naval Air Service and the Royal Flying Corps will preserve and foster that esprit de corps which these two separate forces have created by their splendid deeds.

GEORGE R.I.

1st.April 1918.

The King's Message to the Royal Air Force.

To the Right Hon. Lord Weir, Secretary of State and President of the Air Council.

I N this supreme hour of victory I send greetings and heartfelt congratulations to all ranks of the Royal Air Force. Our aircraft have been ever in the forefront of the battle; pilots and observers have consistently maintained the offensive throughout the ever-changing fortunes of the day, and in the war zones our gallant dead have lain always beyond the enemies' lines or far out to sea.

OUR far-flung squadrons have flown over home waters and foreign seas, the Western and Italian battle lines, Rhineland, the mountains of Macedonia, Gallipoli, Palestine, the plains of Meso- potamia, the forests and swamps of East Africa, the North-West frontier of India, and the deserts of Arabia, Sinai, and Darfur.

THE birth of the Royal Air Force, with its wonderful expansion and development, will ever remain one of the most remarkable achievements of the Great War.

EVERYWHERE, by God's help, officers, men and women of the Royal Air Force have splendidly maintained our just cause, and the value of their assistance to the Navy, the Army, and to Home Defence has been incalculable.   For all their magnificent work, self- sacrifice, and devotion to duty, I ask you on behalf of the Empire to thank them.

November 11th, 1918

George R. I.

Above

Addressed to Lord Weir, the Secretary of State for the Royal Air Force and therefore its most senior representative in the Government, King George V's message was distributed to all serving members of the Royal Air Force and Women's Royal Air Force at the end of the First World War. Besides praising the outstanding achievements of airmen and airwomen serving in every theatre of war, the King also recognised the formation of an independent Royal Air Force as "one of the most remarkable achievements of the Great War". Today the truth of these words is indisputable, but when they were written many senior officers in the Army and Royal Navy were sceptical.

A CENTURY OF ACHIEVEMENT

The RAF has 100 years of history to be proud of, from the heroics of the World Wars
to the peace-keeping and humanitarian operations of the 21st century

In the summer of 1917, a formation of German aircraft flew over London in broad daylight and bombed the city. The resultant public outcry led directly to a recommendation that the British Army's Royal Flying Corps and the Royal Navy's Royal Naval Air Service should be amalgamated and on 1 April 1918 the Royal Air Force, the world's first truly independent air force, came into being. In the remaining months of the First World War it participated in the successful campaign that led to the Armistice.

When the war ended, the RAF was threatened from a different direction and it was only the political skills of Lord Trenchard as Chief of the Air Staff that preserved the new service in the face of calls for its abolition. In early campaigns in British Somaliland and Iraq, the RAF showed itself to be not only an effective fighting force but also an economical one. It was also innovative, mounting the first

aerial evacuation in history when it flew 556 civilians out of Kabul, which was threatened by a civil war, and breaking world height and speed records, as well as making non-stop long-range flights in single-engined aircraft from the UK to South Africa and from Egypt to Australia.

TRAINING THE NEXT GENERATION

Trenchard established the RAF College at Cranwell in Lincolnshire and the Apprentice School at Halton in Buckinghamshire. The latter offered paid apprenticeships and skills for life at a time when there was no welfare state and the majority of poorer children left school at 14. The top three Halton apprentices were sent on to Cranwell, and among those who benefited was one Frank Whittle, who was to pioneer the jet engine. In the 1930s, the RAF was also the first to adopt radar technology and integrate it into an

British Aircraft Corporation Jet Provost T1 aircraft of No.2 Flying Training School, c. 1956

Below: A GR9 Harrier prepares to land on board HMS Ark Royal, 2010

efficient air defence system, which then enabled Fighter Command's immortal "Few" in their Spitfires and Hurricanes to prevail in the Battle of Britain in 1940, the first strategically important battle in history to be fought entirely in the air.

As well as defending the nation against air attack, the service went on to play a major role in helping to ensure the country's vital sea lanes were kept open during the Battle of the Atlantic, then contributing to the ultimately successful campaigns in the Mediterranean and North Africa. Meanwhile, Bomber Command fought its own long and costly campaign to undermine the Third Reich's capacity to make war and paving the way for the D-Day invasion culminating in the collapse of the Nazi regime. In the course of the campaign, bomber crews suffered nearly one in 10 of all the wartime losses sustained by the British armed forces. In the Far East, the RAF recovered from early setbacks in the war with Japan to help in achieving the final victory and bringing to an end the most costly global conflict in human history.

KEEPING THE PEACE

In the immediate post-war period, despite the inevitable reductions from its wartime peak of

"During its century of existence, the RAF has helped to keep the peace from Belize to Baghdad"

nearly 1.2 million men and women, the service, along with the US Air Force, achieved a notable and bloodless early victory of the Cold War when it flew nearly 400,000 tons of supplies into the beleaguered city of Berlin to break the Soviet-imposed blockade and ensure the position of the Western Allies in the city was maintained. In a succession of successful campaigns in the Far and Middle East, from Malaysia, Borneo, and Brunei to Oman and Kuwait, the RAF helped ensure that withdrawal from Empire did not result in the advance of regimes and governments inimical to Britain's interests. At the same time the RAF, through NATO, helped maintain the peace in Western Europe, not least through bearing the responsibility for the UK nuclear deterrent for most of the dangerous decades of the 1950s and '60s.

In more recent times and conflicts, the RAF has played a major part in helping to liberate the Falkland Islands and Kuwait, topple Saddam Hussein and Colonel Gadaffi, and today is striving to contain and roll back the perversion of Islam represented by Da'esh and Al Qaeda. During its century of existence, the RAF has operated in six of the world's seven continents and helped to keep the peace from the Arctic Ocean to the South Atlantic and from Belize to Baghdad. It will continue to do so with the same courage, professionalism and devotion to duty that have been the hallmark of the service since 1918.

Below: An RAF Chinook during the resupply of the men of 42 Commando Royal Marines in Afghanistan, 2007

RAF TIMELINE

Charting the Royal Air Force's landmark events of the past 100 years

1 APRIL 1918

Formation of the RAF and Women's Royal Air Force (below, left)

1918

Major General Sir Hugh Trenchard appointed first Chief of the Air Staff

1918

RAF "Wings" flying badge introduced

1919

An RAF bombing campaign brings the Third Afghan War to an end (below, top right)

1919

The White Paper known as the "Trenchard Memorandum" is introduced in the House of Commons by Winston Churchill

1920

The RAF College at Cranwell opens

1920

The Women's Royal Air Force is disbanded

1920

The first RAF airshow takes place at RAF Hendon (above, bottom right)

1923

The RAF Badge,
authorised by
HM King George V,
is registered

1925

"Pink's War" in India.
The RAF's first campaign
waged purely using
aircraft (below, top left)

1925

The first University Air
Squadron and first
Auxiliary Air Force
Squadron are formed

1929

The Observer Corps
transfers to RAF control
(below, top right)

1931

The RAF wins a third
victory and claims the
Schneider Trophy (above,
bottom left)

1934

The first RAF Expansion
Scheme – A – is approved
by the Cabinet

1937

The first airborne radar is
fitted to a Handley Page
Heyford

1939

The Women's Auxiliary Air
Force (WAAF) is formed
(above, bottom right)

1940

Battle of Britain. The RAF withstands and repulses repeated attacks from the German Luftwaffe (below, top left)

1941

Formation of the Air Training Corps

1941

First successful flight of the Gloster E28/39 Pioneer powered by Whittle's W1 jet engine (below, top right)

1942

The RAF Regiment and Pathfinder Force are formed

1943

Dams Raid. 617 Squadron undertakes low-level attacks against dams in the Ruhr Valley in Germany (above, bottom left)

1944

RAF prisoners-of-war stage a mass breakout from Stalag Luft III

1948–1949

The Berlin Airlift. Soviet forces blockade Berlin leaving aviation as the only way to supply the Allied sections of the divided city (above, bottom right)

1949

The WAAF is renamed the Women's Royal Air Force

1952

Pilot Officer Jean Lennox Bird, WRAF VR, is the first woman to receive RAF pilot's wings (below, left)

1953

The RAF takes delivery of its first atomic bombs

1954

The last operational sortie by an RAF Spitfire

1957

The RAF tests Britain's first thermonuclear weapon in Operation Grapple

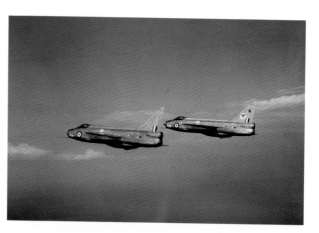

1958

The Firestreak air-to-air missile and Bloodhound surface-to-air missile, the first of their type, enter service

1960

The Lightning, the first RAF fighter aircraft capable of flying at over twice the speed of sound, enters service (above, top right)

1962

The RAF initiates a permanent nuclear quick reaction alert force

1963

The Ballistic Missile Early Warning Station at RAF Fylingdales is operational (above, bottom right)

1965

The Red Arrows flying display team is formed (below, left)

1966

The Supply Control Centre opens at RAF Hendon

1969

Responsibility for Britain's strategic nuclear deterrent passes from the RAF to the Royal Navy

1973

RAF Support Command is formed

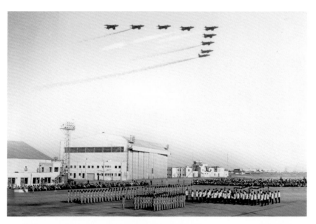

1974

Successful launch of Skynet 2B communications satellite, part of the British Military Satellite Communications project

1974

RAF evacuates British civilians from Cyprus

1979

The RAF withdraws from Malta after 60 years (above, top right)

1982

An RAF Vulcan attacks Port Stanley Airfield (above, bottom right)

1984

The RAF takes part in Operation Bushel delivering famine relief to Ethiopia (below, top left)

1986

RAF Marine Branch is disbanded

1987

First award of the Queen's medal to a female RAF officer

1989

The RAF allows female aircrew to be employed in all non-combat roles

1990

The RAF deploys to the Gulf after Iraq invades Kuwait (above, bottom left)

1991

Julie Gibson becomes the first female regular officer to graduate as an RAF pilot (above, right)

1994

The WRAF and RAF formally merge

1996

The first woman joins the RAF Regiment

1998

The RAF transports
casualties from the
Omagh bombing
to hospitals

2001

RAF operations commence
in Afghanistan, with
Harriers arriving in 2004
(below, top left)

2001

The first British pilot flies a
prototype of the Lockheed
Martin F-35B

2002

3,000 RAF personnel
provide cover during
a Fire Brigade Union
dispute

2004

RAF crews train with the
US Air Force for RPAS
operations

2005

The Battle of Britain
Monument is opened
in London (above,
bottom left)

2006

The RAF introduces a new
command structure

2007

The RAF provides
UK flood relief

2008

Flight Lieutenant Michelle Goodman is the first female DFC recipient

2011

The RAF is involved in the evacuation of civilians followed by combat operations in Libya (opposite, bottom right)

2012

The Bomber Command Memorial opens in London's Green Park (opposite, top right)

2014

Operation Shader commences with air strikes against the Islamic State group in Iraq (below, top right)

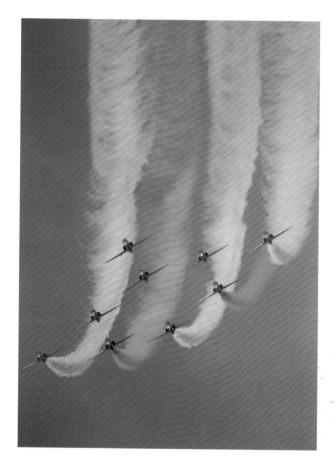

2015

The last RAF Search and Rescue mission

2016

The Red Arrows fly over China for the first time (above, left)

2017

The RAF opens all its roles to female recruits (above, bottom right)

2018

The RAF celebrates its 100th birthday

A FORCE FOR GOOD

The RAF100 Appeal provides a breadth of benefits, from supporting current and former personnel to nurturing the service of the future

The Royal Air Force has a wide global community, all rooted in excellence in aviation across 100 years of service to the UK, the Commonwealth and our allies. Conceived and proven through the need to protect these islands in the greatest conflicts of the 20th century, the RAF has since grown in scope, capability and mission, defending the values of democracy and the rule of law worldwide with integrity, determination and unparalleled skill.

In this centenary year, the RAF100 Appeal has a significant role to play. Maggie Appleton, who is Chief Executive of the RAF Museum and is on the Appeal Board, is well placed to assess how 100 years of history inform the modern-day RAF. "The RAF100 Appeal is both a part of and a support to the RAF100 programme," she says. "The focus of this programme is to commemorate, celebrate and inspire. Those are three really important strands because, while it's important to give thanks for 100 years of achievement and sacrifice, it's a celebration of the professionalism of today's serving personnel and also – something that is so important to the RAF and Appeal partners – thinking about how we look to the future and how we inspire the generations to come."

CAUSE AND EFFECT

The RAF100 Appeal brings together five partners: the RAF Benevolent Fund, RAF Association, RAF Charitable Trust, RAF Museum and the Royal Air Force itself. The Appeal Board comprises a trustee and the chief executive of the four key charities, two representatives from the RAF and two independent trustees. For Appleton, the process is underpinned by a spirit of collegiate cooperation. "We share the work together as a partnership and play to all our strengths," she says, "working with the governance of the charities, on the events and on the fundraising, publications and merchandising, keeping each other up to date and supported."

Maggie Appleton has been the RAF Museum's CEO since 2014, having started her career at the Royal Armouries and worked in community museums in Stevenage and Luton before becoming CEO of Luton Culture. She remembers visiting with her own (now grown-up) children and has always had an affinity with the RAF – her father having served as an armourer on Lancasters for 57 Squadron during the Second World War.

Appleton shares the RAF's passion to inspire the next generation, and believes that the Appeal can have a lasting effect on the wider community. "Just before Christmas, we had a big STEM [science, technology, engineering and mathematics] launch at the Museum's Cosford site, to encourage work with schools and young people," she says. "We had a couple of hundred pupils from West Midlands schools learning about different scientific principles and techniques – really hands-on, fun examples for good practical engagement. It's our role to flick that switch on at primary school age and get children thinking, 'Yes, I'm keen on science. And it's really exciting what I've learned. I could do this'."

Below: The RAF Museum's Chief Executive Maggie Appleton

Opposite: The Museum has undergone an impressive transformation

BRIGHT PROSPECTS

Getting children engaged and retained in maths and science to A level and beyond is a perennial problem for UK schools and, despite STEM initiatives raising numbers in recent years, a government Green Paper in 2017 cited research claiming 40 per cent of UK employers have problems recruiting staff with relevant STEM skills. This supports the anecdotal evidence that there is plenty of work still to be done.

"The lack of numbers coming through the workforce is a massive issue for our defence industry partners, as well as for the RAF," says Appleton. "There isn't just one silver bullet – it has to be on a number of levels." It's why, as part of the centenary, the RAF has launched the Trenchard Group, a wide-ranging platform of practical initiatives to attract and retain young people in STEM subjects and help them see the air force as a viable career option.

That it should be named after the "Father of the Royal Air Force", Viscount Trenchard, is more than a mere nod to history. Innovation and technical expertise have been at the heart of the RAF's mission since 1918. When aeroplanes were first pressed into military service, they demanded the utmost bravery of pilots operating at the very edge of technology. The Battle of Britain was decided not just by skill and courage, but by the marginal design and performance gains of the Spitfire and Hurricane over Germany's highly capable ME-109. And today's challenges range from cyber-attack and surveillance to the development of pioneering thermal paint to protect aircraft carriers from the extreme heat of a new generation of vertical-landing stealth fighters. In short, we need brains. "We absolutely need to support young people into these industries," says Appleton. "It's the only way to keep the RAF – and UK plc – ahead of the curve."

The Trenchard Group scheme aims to foster innovative thinking through its own three strands of development – ideas, scholarships and pathways – offering what it calls "a full spectrum of training, education and conceptual development for anyone to anywhere". This includes a new think tank on air power, academic placements, flying scholarships, and professional and leadership routes mapped out "from air cadet to air marshal".

None of this works, however, without awareness. The RAF100 events and the associated Appeal are bringing to a wider audience the importance of education, plus greater visibility for those current and former forces personnel who play such a vital role in our national story. "It's about using this landmark anniversary to start a national conversation about the RAF," says Appleton, "in terms of awareness and understanding about what it does, what it's achieved and how it's affected all of our lives."

PLENTY TO CELEBRATE

The centrepiece of the celebration takes place on 10 July, with a centenary service in Westminster Abbey, followed by a parade in The Mall and mass flypast. The Museum will be supporting the public display on Horse Guards Parade and the RAF100 national tour with the provision of aircraft such as the Sopwith Snipe and the Harrier GR3. "It's a chance to show off the best of the service," says Appleton, "whether that's through air shows or

"It's a chance to show off the best of the service, a great opportunity for people to interact with the RAF"

themed regional events. It's a great opportunity for people to interact with the RAF."

Alongside the RAF100 event programme, the RAF Museum is collecting oral histories that will be shared in new exhibitions and online. Interviews are with serving personnel, as well as veterans and the broader supporting RAF Family. This extraordinary community is supported by all the RAF100 Appeal charities: the RAF Association, Benevolent Fund, Charitable Trust and the Museum.

"It's important to think about how society has changed over the past hundred years and how our freedoms are, and have been, protected every day by our military personnel," says Appleton. "Much of the work that will be funded by the Appeal is thinking about families and veterans, and how we support people who have been in the RAF to flourish and lead interesting and fulfilling lives post-service. So it's a cradle-to-grave piece of thinking. For us at the Museum, much of our input is about telling the story of the broader RAF family, which has changed beyond recognition in the past 10 or 20 years. It's much broader than those who are directly employed, because there are civilians working for the RAF and industry

*Left: The RAF100 Appeal
will support service personnel
past and present*

partners in the supply chain, working together, many of them on RAF bases."

THE NEXT CHAPTER

This, for Appleton, is the key to legacy for the RAF100 Appeal – to ensure deeper, long-lasting relationships beyond 2018. She says key sponsors such as BAE Systems, Babcock and Fujitsu will no longer see themselves as working in parallel with the RAF but as part of a wider organisation. "A complex but exciting ecosystem," as she puts it. "One that benefits from shared expertise and pathways to unlock the skills of our youngsters."

Up to a certain level, funds raised by the Appeal will be shared equally between the five partners. Beyond that, there will be opportunities for grant applications to be made.

It's a hugely complicated task to marshal the multiple facets of the RAF100 Appeal effectively, not least for Appleton as – when interviewed for this article – she was in the midst of a complete transformation of the Museum's London site for its re-opening on 30 June.

"We've got three new exhibitions and we've been transforming the landscape of the site, so it's really been all hands to the pump," she says. "We're proud of the work that's been put in over the past months and years, and we're be full of exhilaration and exhaustion in equal measure. But we're ready to go!"

This level of commitment is being mirrored right across the RAF100 Appeal and thus promises to support the force's wider family, providing a practical legacy for an exciting and innovative new century of service.

FULL STEM AHEAD

With an eye to its next 100 years, the RAF is giving children a step up in the world of Science, Technology, Engineering and Maths. By Wing Commanders Glynis Dean and Russ Barnes

Since its inception in 1918, the Royal Air Force has constantly pushed the boundaries of innovation. The service is credited with the invention of the jet engine, which ushered in a new era of flight. The pioneering use of radar gave the RAF a decisive advantage in the Battle of Britain, and the RAF led the way in developing accurate navigation, guidance and targeting systems whose principles are still applied today. The RAF's ongoing quest to fly faster, higher and for longer, with ever-increasing agility and flexibility, means that the UK's security remains protected by one of the most modern and best equipped air forces in the world.

This spirit of relentless innovation is as strong today as it was 100 years ago. RAF servicemen and women are pioneers and innovators, working at the cutting edge of technology. The RAF operates some of the most advanced military aircraft in the world including the Typhoon, Puma Mk2, Atlas A400M and, coming into service shortly, the F-35 Lightning II and P-8A Poseidon. In 2018, the RAF launched its first imaging satellite, capable of delivering high-quality imagery and 3D video from space. Looking to the future, the RAF will harness new leading-edge technology to further exploit the possibilities of space, develop operational capabilities in cyberspace and adopt new techniques using artificial intelligence, augmented reality and simulation.

Maintaining its position as a world-class air force depends on attracting high-calibre men and women with vision, imagination and passion. The RAF's centenary is an opportunity to inspire and influence the next generation of innovators, aviators and engineers to realise their potential and make their mark in projecting the service into its second century.

THE STEM ZONE

The RAF100 national tour of the UK features an immersive and interactive STEM (Science, Technology, Engineering and Maths) Zone among its key attractions. Under the RAF100 Inspire banner, and in partnership with colleagues from the defence and aerospace industries, the STEM Zone exposes visitors to the wonders of virtual and augmented reality, and offers engaging challenges themed around quadcopters, cyber security, coding and much more. By showcasing modern technology and innovation, our aim is to stimulate future generations and open minds to the breadth of choice and opportunity that is accessible to young people today.

With more than 80 per cent of its roles requiring STEM skills and with over 50 per cent of the workforce being engineers, the RAF is committed, with its partners in academia and industry, to addressing the national skills shortages, particularly in engineering.

As part of the centenary celebrations, the service is delivering the most ambitious early-years programme ever undertaken in defence – worth £2 million and aiming to reach two million young people between the ages of 9 and 14. Specifically designed with inclusion and fair access at its heart, it recognises that enthusing students about maths and science – and busting damaging stereotyping based on gender, ethnicity and background – must begin early: the earlier the better.

So, for the first time, the RAF has developed primary-school activities directed towards the transition between primary and secondary levels of education when the impact of such misperception is felt most keenly, as well as expanding massively its already-mature programme for secondary students and youth groups such as the Air Cadet Organisation and the Scouts.

The activities include a challenging mix of maths, physics, engineering and logistics-focused, hands-on activity and curriculum-linked, online resources. Participating students also meet RAF role models, offering real-life insight and context to academic studies and a glimpse into the STEM careers spectrum. Development and delivery of the programme has been made possible through the support and partnership of industrial, academic and charity partners and by the commitment of the RAF's 500-plus STEM Ambassador network.

A RANGE OF ACTIVITIES

Key elements of the programme include "Primary School STEM in a Box". This has been developed in partnership with the Royal Academy of Engineering and comprises an activity box and stand-alone teaching resources. It tracks the iconic technological inventions through the first 10 decades of the RAF's history that have seen it continue to operate at the leading edge of technology. Boxes will be offered to 1,000 schools across the UK. The activities include aircraft design, radar, ejector seats, stealth and space. This inventive, colourful learning resource package, aptly named "Aiming for Awesome" is fully downloadable.

There is also a Primary School Activity Book packed with puzzles, word searches and other fun resources, which has been made available online to 26,000 primary schools throughout the UK (including a Welsh-language version), and, in addition, there is a competition seeking innovative solutions to the question of Future Flight.

The National Robotics Challenge is delivered to secondary students in years 7 to 9 and involves the design and building of robots and their programming to meet a series of tough, time-constrained challenges to be completed on a specially designed, airfield-based activity board. The project has attracted entries from over 400 schools in 2018, involving more than 10,000 students. The national final was held at the Big Bang Science and Engineering Fair at the Birmingham NEC in March.

SCHOOL VISITS

The RAF is also embarking on STEM Days, delivered in 100 schools to whole year groups and to youth organisations. These comprise a series of hands-on engineering-based activities including robotics and an aircraft design and build challenge. More than 15,000 young people will benefit in the coming academic year with over 10,000 of them receiving the new Industrial Cadet Challenger Award.

STEM Residential Courses at RAF units across the UK will offer over 460 students a unique engineering or logistics opportunity. Open to students age 14 or 15, these week-long courses are delivered by RAF engineers and logisticians and supported by education and industrial partners. The courses provide a high-tempo, demanding mix of hands-on activity underpinned by maths and science learning, against the backdrop of the RAF lived-experience. Participating students earn silver-level, British Science Association CREST Awards and silver-level Industrial Cadet Awards.

SCOUT'S HONOUR

The RAF has also commenced a three-year partnership with the Scouts through sponsorship of the Air Researcher Badge, which promotes aviation and aerospace through badge learning.

Other elements of the Youth STEM Programme include the Schools STEM Roadshow, called "It's All About Numbers", delivered in partnership with BAE Systems and the Royal Navy to more than 100,000 years 7 and 8 students. In Scotland, there is the Primary Engineer competition, where more than 15,000 students have entered their innovative solutions to real-life problems by asking themselves "What would I do if I was an engineer?"

This programme will form the core of the RAF100 inspire legacy for the next generation. The activities delivered under RAF100 will ensure that the RAF remains in the mind of many of these young people as they continue their educational journeys, and so help the RAF retain its position as an organisation focussed on sustaining its lifeblood – a steady flow of skilled, innovative and highly motivated young people.

"The Royal Air Force's focus has always been on the future, and so the legacy of RAF100 must be a springboard into our next century," says the RAF100 STEM Champion from AOC 38 Group. "We will ignite young people's passion for air, space, cyber and engineering, helping everyone to fulfil their potential."

Opposite and left: The RAF's host of STEM initiatives are providing the next generation with insight and inspiration

BACK TO SCHOOL

RAF100's Chief Operating Officer Zerrin Lovett sheds light on the
ideas and inspiration behind the RAF100 Schools project

*You have created an interesting educational programme
as part of the RAF's centenary – what was the thinking
behind this?*
Zerrin Lovett: When I first took on the role of Chief
Operating Officer I was challenged to develop a
programme that engaged with the under 25s. I did some
research and decided that education would be an excellent
way in which to reach out to children.

*The subjects of history and physics are not often rolled out
together in schools or with youth groups, yet this is exactly
what this new project for RAF100 does. What inspired
the unusual decision to explore the history of the RAF
through technology?*
ZL: Having served in the RAF myself I am incredibly proud
of our history and wanted to give children the opportunity
to learn about it. I was in the process of putting together
the "Inspire" package with RAF College Cranwell and it
occurred to me that the RAF was created because of
technology and has driven technological advances
throughout its history. Did you know that an RAF engineer
invented the jet engine and because of that we can all go
on holiday in large aircraft? Also, the creation of radar as
we know it today was improved to help protect the UK in
the Second World War. It helped with the Battle of Britain
and again ensures that airlines are safe when they fly
around the world today.

So how did you go about this?
ZL: We partnered with the Historical Association and the
Institute of Physics to deliver the RAF100 Schools project.
I met with both organisations and they embraced the
opportunity to work together. It is something that neither
have done before; I must thank Becky Sullivan and Paula
Kitching from the Historical Association and Charles Tracy
and Taj Bhutta from the Institute of Physics, whose hard
work made the project happen. Wing Commanders Glynis

Dean and Russ Barnes worked extremely hard to bring
together the RAF's contribution and managed the project
for me.

What does it look like?
ZL: We have created a website – www.raf100schools.org.uk
– which is a free digital resource for ages 8 to 18 years
and beyond. The project aims to give young people a far
greater understanding of the role that the RAF and its
people have played in UK history, and how it and they have
helped to shape the world we now live in.

The purpose-built RAF100 Schools website contains
activities, information and enquiries to bring history and
STEM (Science, Technology, Engineering and Maths) themes
together in an exciting and new way. Eight specially made
short films introduce the topics of Origins and Aircraft
Design; The Battle of Britain and Radar; Codebreakers and
Communication; Relief Operations and Airdrops; The Jet
Age and Helicopters; Aerial Reconnaissance and Stereo
Images; the Falklands War and Navigation; and Medicine,
War and Rescue.

Of huge significance are two interactive maps that
plot every location where the RAF operated from 1916,
starting with the Royal Flying Corps (RFC) and the Royal
Navy Air Service (RNAS), through to the modern day
in the UK and overseas. The maps can be added to by
schools, groups and individuals to build up a picture of
life and scientific discovery at these sites that once dotted
the whole of the UK.

Is it just available this year?
ZL: The project was created for the centenary but the
resources and content will last for many years to come,
helping to provide an important legacy for RAF100. So many
children have had family members who were or are in the
RAF and I want to give them the opportunity to learn a little
about the important role they have played.

PASSING ON THE CENTENARY MESSAGE

The RAF100 Baton Relay has visited 100 significant sites far and wide, inspiring as it goes

One of the most exciting celebratory events that took place this year was the RAF100 Baton Relay, which saw a specially designed baton visit 100 sites associated with the RAF in 100 days. The relay began its journey at the Royal Courts of Justice on 1 April 2018 and ends on 10 July on Horse Guards Parade, having visited every region of the UK and several overseas operational theatres along the way.

"I am delighted that what started as a simple orienteering challenge, conceived on one of my training runs almost two years ago, has grown into one of the most inclusive and far-reaching RAF100 endeavours," says Group Captain Rob Woods, the senior officer responsible for the Baton Relay. "From the outset,

I had two simple principles: firstly, that the baton should support the objectives of RAF100 in order to commemorate, celebrate and inspire; and secondly, to take the baton as far and wide possible, both in the United Kingdom and at locations overseas where RAF personnel are deployed on operations."

A FAMILY AFFAIR

Personnel from across the RAF family – including regulars, reservists, civil servants, contractors, air cadets and family members – have been participating in the relay, which was originally the inspiration of the RAF Orienteering Association. The orienteering principles of navigation and physical challenge remain at the heart of the relay, but the orienteers are now being supported by members of 20 other RAF sports associations showcasing talent and endeavour in numerous disciplines.

Flying Officer Kurt Lee was involved in the launch of the Baton Relay. "As a Malaysian national serving in the Royal Air Force and representing the Commonwealth it was an absolute honour to be one of the starting runners of the Baton Relay," he says. "The highlight for me was meeting and hearing the stories of former prisoner of war Air Commodore Charles Clarke, who was part of the 'Great Escape', and Wing Commander Paul Farnes, one of 'The Few' to whom we owe so much."

The baton was designed and constructed by apprentices and staff at No.4 School of Technical Training, MOD St Athan, with support from RAF100 technology partners Raytheon. There is a large amount of symbolism built into it. It is constructed from three materials that have featured in aircraft construction during the past 100 years: wood, brass and aluminium. The angle of the top of the baton is exactly 22 degrees, acknowledging that the technical training school is

part of 22 Group, now responsible for all RAF training activity. The ring of eight lights around the top of the handle commemorates the Lancasters of 617 Squadron that did not return from the famous Dam Busters mission.

"It's been a huge privilege to be part of the team that designed and built the baton," says Squadron Leader Gareth Thomas, Officer Commanding No.4 School of Technical Training, MOD St Athan. "Creating an object that would be both a thing of beauty and serve as an inspiration to our next generation was at the heart of our aim when we started the project a year ago. It has become an icon of RAF100 and a real showcase for RAF engineering and craftsmanship at its very finest."

INSPIRING EXCITEMENT

Squadron Leader Daniela Nowalski is the Baton Relay Chief of Staff, and the only full-time member of the planning team, who had the privilege of taking the baton to the Shetland Islands. "To achieve our aim to visit every operational site in the UK it was planned to carry the baton in a Typhoon from RAF Lossiemouth over our

remote radar head at Saxa Vord on Unst, with a detour over Bell's Brae Primary School in Lerwick," she says. "I'd spent the early part of the afternoon speaking to the children in classrooms and when the time came to head outside they were beyond excited. When the aircraft flew over a second time some of the 300 pupils were screaming like it was a pop concert. It's safe to say there were some inspired young people – their excitement audible over the roar of the aircraft!"

The Baton Relay promotes the three main aims of RAF100 – to commemorate, celebrate and inspire. It involves veterans and visits historic locations to commemorate the service's past; it showcases opportunities for sport within the RAF to celebrate the achievements of its personnel; and it strives to inspire younger generations, especially those from harder-to-reach communities.

Opposite: The baton arrives at the RAF Museum London at the end of the first of its 100-day journey

Above: Flight Lieutenant Lucy Nell leads a team of runners past the Cenotaph in central London

"Creating an object that would be both a thing of beauty and serve as an inspiration to our next generation was at the heart of our aim when we started the project a year ago"

WOMEN OF THE RAF

Over the past century, the responsibilities of women in the RAF have grown to the point where every role is now open to male and female personnel alike

Over the last hundred years, the role of women within society has changed radically. During wartime, vital support roles were undertaken so that men could be released for combat. Today, women are serving permanently in their own right.

During the First and Second World Wars, women serving with Britain's Armed Forces contributed greatly to the country's war effort and in doing so broke down social gender stereotypes. Given the opportunity and training they proved that women could successfully undertake male military roles under difficult circumstances.

The Women's Royal Air Force (WRAF) was created on 1 April, 1918 (the same day as the RAF) and disbanded in 1920. Princess Mary's Royal Air Force Nursing Service was established as a permanent branch of the Royal Air Force in 1923. The Women's Auxiliary Air Force (WAAF), formed for war in 1939, was continued after the Second World War ended. It was re-formed as the WRAF, a permanent female peacetime force in 1949 and was fully integrated into the RAF in 1994.

One key figure in the history of women in the RAF is Dame Helen Gwynne-Vaughan. A formidable leader and inspirational speaker, she laid the foundations and set the standards for all women's air services. During the First World War, Gwynne-Vaughan was invited by the War Office, along with Mrs Chalmers Watson, to help form the Women's Army Auxiliary Corps (WAAC). As Chief Controller stationed in France, she was instrumental in creating a respected and disciplined force.

As a result of her success with the WAAC, Gwynne-Vaughan was transferred to the WRAF in September 1918. Given the powers of a Brigadier, she began the task of reorganisation. In a short space of time, she revised the standing orders, overhauled the administrative system, opened and equipped Berridge House in Hampstead for the training of officers, authorised the new blue uniform and introduced military protocol. Her professionalism helped change male attitudes towards women in the air service.

In 1935, Gwynne-Vaughan played a pivotal role in forming the Emergency Services, an organisation established to train female officers. In September 1938, with war once again on the horizon, the Auxiliary Territorial Service (ATS), the women's branch of the British Army, was created. Gwynne-Vaughan was appointed Director, the position that she held until her retirement from military service in 1941.

"By the end of the year the WRAF was the best disciplined and best turned-out women's organisation in the country," said Air Vice Marshal Sir William Sefton Brancker, a pioneering figure in British aviation. "This remarkable achievement was due to Dame Helen Gwynne-Vaughan."

A NEW WARTIME ROLE

On 28 June 1939, King George VI established the WAAF for duty with the RAF in time of war. Since 1938, RAF Companies had existed within the ATS, the female force equivalent to the Territorial Army. These companies were affiliated to Royal Auxiliary Air Force squadrons but, by May 1939, the government decided that a separate women's air service was necessary.

The WAAF was not an independent organisation, nor was it completely integrated within the RAF. Rather, it was interlinked with its "parent" force for the purpose of substituting, where possible, women for RAF personnel. It was mobilised on 28 August 1939 and, within the year, tens of thousands of women had volunteered to serve.

In 1941, the WAAF became part of the Armed Forces of the Crown, subject to the Air Force Act. This was greeted with pride and enthusiasm by its members. With conscription for women introduced from December 1941, the ranks swelled further. No fewer than 183,317 women volunteered with a further 33,932 called up. The majority were aged between 18 and 40, and they came from all walks of life and from around the world. By 1943, 48 nationalities were represented in the force including Irish, Caribbean and Polish women. By 1945 a quarter of a million women had served in the WAAF in over 110 different trades, supporting operations around the world. They were an integral and vital part of the RAF's war effort.

With war coming to an end, demobilisation began. By June 1946, more than 100,000 women had left the service. The Government was conscious of the contribution made by the WAAF and proposals for retaining a permanent female peacetime force were discussed. As a result, the Women's Royal Air Force was re-formed on 1 February 1949.

A VITAL CONTRIBUTION

Despite organisational differences, including a separate ranking system and pay that was two thirds of their RAF colleagues, these women realised they were integral to the RAF. The initial scepticism and humour that greeted many WAAFs soon turned to respect and admiration as female personnel proved time and again their dedication and skill. Day in, day out, they diligently did their duty. Great strength of character was required by many WAAFs in continuing to work despite the loss of friends and loved ones.

Many WAAFs were decorated for their gallantry. Daphne Pearson, a medical corporal, rescued a pilot from his crashed aircraft at RAF Detling on 31 May 1940. As the aircraft and its bomb load exploded, Corporal Pearson threw herself on top of the pilot to protect him from the blast and splinters. As a result of her action, Corporal Pearson was awarded the George Cross.

The women of the WAAF were a vital part of the RAF's war effort and through their example demonstrated the contribution that women could make to Britain's Armed

Above: Dame Helen Gwynne-Vaughan
(left) and the first director of the WRAF,
Dame Felicity Hanbury

Opposite: Members of the WAAF assist
with rearming Lancaster bombers

"Within the year, tens of thousands of women had volunteered to serve"

Forces. The work undertaken by the WAAF was wide ranging: from cooking and meteorology, to administrative duties, and maintaining and repairing aircraft. Women replaced RAF personnel in those trades where there were shortages. There was an ebb and flow of requirements, but safety and physical wellbeing were primary concerns. Except for nursing orderlies, aircrew duty was not approved for women. They did fly aircraft in Britain during the Second World War, but they did so as civilian pilots of the Air Transport Auxiliary.

The success of the WAAF was due, in part, to it being interlinked with the RAF, but difficulties did arise. WAAF officers were not able to command RAF personnel until after the WAAF became an element of the Armed Forces of the Crown in 1941. Once this took place, further roles became open to them. In 1944, for example, the first female station commander was appointed.

Officers and airwomen were selected by interview prior to training. Some trades required several weeks' attendance at specialised schools before posting took place. Certain work, such as code and cipher duty, was restricted to officers. Particular trades needed suitable qualifications, such as a relevant degree. Overseas service was available to officers from 1940, but only to airwomen from 1943 onwards. The practical work undertaken by the WAAF, combined with the intangible comfort and moral support they provided to their RAF colleagues, was essential in keeping the RAF flying.

RETURN OF THE WRAF

The Women's Royal Air Force was reborn on 1 February 1949, offering women a full professional career in the Air Force for the first time. Although women had served alongside the RAF before, it had always been in a temporary wartime capacity.

Below: Recruitment posters for the WAAF (left) and the WRAF

The passing of the Army and Air Force (Women's Service) Act in 1948 created the opportunity for a permanent peacetime role for women in the Armed Forces, in recognition of their invaluable wartime contribution.

From the outset, the WRAF was to be integrated as fully as possible with the RAF, a source of much pride for its members. All new entrants were commissioned or enlisted in the RAF, taking the same oath as the men, and subject to the same conditions of service and disciplinary code. The only restriction placed on their employment was that they should not undertake combatant duties. King's Regulations were rewritten to include the WRAF and, except in issues of women's welfare, WRAF personnel were in principle to be treated like their male counterparts.

Initially, female entrants underwent basic training separately, joining their male colleagues for professional training in their chosen branch or trade. On completion of training, WRAF personnel were posted to RAF stations both at home and overseas, serving as far afield as Singapore, Burma and Iraq. Despite their non-combatant status, the WRAF found themselves at the heart of Britain's numerous post-war conflicts in places such as Malaya, Kenya and Cyprus, where they performed vital support roles, often in dangerous situations.

From 1949, around 80 per cent of trades were open to women, including driving, ground signalling, clerical work and catering. Opportunities to fly existed for members of the WRAF Volunteer Reserve, but regulars were not yet accepted as aircrew. In time, more technical trades became available such as mechanic and air traffic control. In 1959, the new trade of Air Quartermaster was opened to women, and by 1962 these became the first females to be recognised as aircrew.

The WRAF and the RAF grew ever closer over the following years and, in 1968, female officers adopted the rank titles of their RAF counterparts. Training was also consolidated both at recruit and officer level and, in 1970, the first female entrants were admitted into the RAF College, Cranwell. Soon after, women began to be promoted to senior appointments and, in 1975, Group Captain Joan Peck became Deputy Director of the Signals Branch, the first woman to hold such a position.

Despite such breakthroughs, the majority of women remained firmly on the ground. It would be over 10 years before the concept of operational female aircrew became a reality. In September 1989, the first female navigators commenced training at RAF Finningley, graduating in 1990 to take up posts in the Hercules fleet. Just five months

Left: As of last year, all roles in the RAF are open to women

later, Flight Lieutenant Julie Gibson became the RAF's first operational female pilot, flying Andovers and the multi-engine Hercules transport.

BREAKING THROUGH

In 1994, women served in all branches of the RAF with the exception of the RAF Regiment. Ninety-six per cent of RAF jobs were open to women – the highest proportion in any of the British Armed Forces. The majority of women were employed in administrative and technical ground trades, but an increasing number were involved in operations.

That year, Flight Lieutenant Jo Salter broke new ground by becoming the first operational fast jet pilot, flying Tornados with 617 Squadron. Since then, female pilots have flown operationally in various theatres, including Afghanistan and Iraq. The impact of their contribution was highlighted when, on 7 March 2008, Flight Lieutenant Michelle Goodman became the first woman to be awarded the Distinguished Flying Cross. In March 2009, Flight Lieutenant Kirsty Moore of 13 Squadron was appointed the first female pilot in the

Red Arrows. Other firsts for women followed. In August 2013, Elaine West was appointed as Director of Projects and Programme Delivery at the Defence Infrastructure Organisation in the rank of Air-Vice Marshal (the first regular service AVM), and in December 2013 Sue Gray was appointed Director of Combat Air Defence, Defence Equipment and Support in the rank of Air-Vice Marshal.

In September 2017, in what was widely considered a defining moment, the RAF became the first British military service to open up all roles to men and women. Women who want to join the RAF Regiment for "Ground Close Combat" roles are now entitled to apply, meaning that there are no longer any RAF roles that exclude women from participation.

"We want the best and most talented individuals to join the Air Force, regardless of their gender, race, or background," said Chief of the Air Staff, Air Chief Marshal Sir Stephen Hillier. "A diverse force is a more effective force, and we need the best people to deliver the important work we do, be it defeating Da'esh in Iraq and Syria, or protecting Britain's skies."

THE CHALLENGE AHEAD

Air Chief Marshal Sir Stephen Hillier reflects on the origins
of the service, and on its future role and objectives

We celebrate the 100th anniversary of the formation of
the Royal Air Force, the world's oldest independent air
arm. The formation of the RAF in 1918 was the culmination
of rapidly growing wartime experience, and of a vision.
That vision was based on the evidence, from the most
terrible war the world had yet experienced, that a new
form of warfare – war in the third dimension – had
emerged, and that it would continue growing rapidly
and become decisive in any future conflict.

It was a vision also based on the realisation that the
ability to fight and win in the air was important in itself,
with an existence that was beyond just providing direct
support to navies and armies. And most importantly in
relation to this anniversary, was the belief that success
in air warfare, whether in 1918 or looking into the future,
would most effectively and efficiently be achieved by a
unified and independent air arm – what would become
the RAF.

THE ORIGINS OF THE RAF

The formation of the RAF was not simply a matter of
improving military effectiveness at a time of immense
courage and sacrifice on the Western Front. One hundred
years ago, on the home front, formations of German
Gotha bombers were dropping bombs, unopposed and
in daylight, on London and other towns and cities in the
south and east of the UK. Many civilians were being killed
and the physical scars can still be seen today. But the
psychological damage to a nation insulated for centuries
against attack by geography and the Royal Navy was far
greater. Air warfare had exposed a critical vulnerability;
warfare was never going to be the same again and
something had to be done.

Previous attempts to unite the efforts of the Admiralty
and the War Office in improving and cohering air
capabilities had proved ineffective. Prime Minister David
Lloyd George therefore acted swiftly and appointed a

"Of at least equal importance to the facts has been the spirit, ethos and character of the service"

Opposite: Air Chief Marshal Sir Stephen Hillier, Chief of the Air Staff

Below: One of the key aims of RAF100 is to inspire the next generation

Cabinet Committee to investigate not just the air defence of London, but how to organise the nation's air power. Within a month, the principal report had recommended that "we must create ... a new Ministry and Air Staff which can properly handle this new instrument of offence, and equip it with the best brains at our disposal for the purpose". The path to the formation of the RAF – an act also of bold, inspirational and visionary political leadership – was assured.

The Air Ministry was formed on 3 January 1918 and the RAF itself on 1 April 1918. The RAF rapidly became the world's most formidable air force, with 22,647 aircraft, 103 airships, 133 squadrons and 15 flights overseas. By the end of the First World War, the RAF had more than 300,000 men and women. By the peak in the Second World War, there were over one million in the RAF with 487 squadrons, engaged continuously with the enemy in every theatre of war, from the first day to the last. The vision of 1918 that air warfare would become decisive, and the efficiency and effectiveness of a unified air force, had been vindicated in the most emphatic terms possible, and has continued to be in every conflict since.

This is the history of the formation of the RAF, but of at least equal importance to the facts has been the spirit,

"The willingness and ability to innovate, adapt and improve has always been an essential part of the RAF story"

ethos and character of the service. From the very start it was conceived and regarded as different to the other services. The founding members of the RAF were pioneers, exploiting a new environment and at the cutting edge of innovation and the latest technology of the day.

The new service sought out talented, innovative and ambitious men and women who were either already highly skilled or had potential that could be unlocked. With so much talent at all levels, it was also a service with a less hierarchical, less deferential outlook on life – one where every individual was valued and judged on merit alone. The first Chief of the Air Staff, Lord Hugh Trenchard, said "We open … widely and to all." It is a principle that continues to be our very essence as an organisation today.

100 YEARS AND COUNTING

Our RAF Centenary Programme, RAF100, embraces that egalitarian spirit. We commemorate the precious legacy of extraordinary success, achievement and sacrifice that is at the heart of the proud tradition and ethos of our service – something that continues to inspire everyone in the RAF

today. We celebrate the skill, professionalism and achievement of the people in today's RAF, airborne every hour of every day, protecting the UK's interests at home and abroad. Perhaps most importantly of all, we will, as we have always done, aim through RAF100 to inspire the next generation. Our focus has always been on the future and the legacy of RAF100 as a launch pad into our second century. We aim to ignite young people's passion for air, space and cyber through science, technology, engineering, art and design, and mathematics programmes and institutions, reaching out to students from all backgrounds, demonstrating that we remain a dynamic engine of social mobility, where everyone can fulfil their true potential. We will also promote the importance of our aerospace and technological industries, whose support is as vital to our operational effectiveness today as it was in 1918, and who help us secure our technological cutting edge for the future. The final important part of our centenary will be the RAF100 Appeal, involving the RAF Benevolent Fund, RAF Association, RAF Charitable Trust and RAF Museum. Together, these charities help protect our precious heritage

Right: The RAF100 Appeal will help support members of the RAF Family, serving and retired

Opposite: The F-35B Lightning represents a significant part of the RAF's future capability

and look after every member of the RAF Family, serving and retired, families and dependants.

As the RAF heads into its second century, what lies ahead? The RAF has been extraordinarily busy and successful on operations across the world for the last three decades, but risks and threats are increasing again, and the character of the conflicts we can expect to fight is changing too. Our extensive operational experience has consistently confirmed the need for the full breadth of air-power capabilities: control of the air and space, precision strike, ISTAR (intelligence, surveillance, target acquisition and reconnaissance) and air mobility. It has also confirmed the need for those capabilities to be at high readiness, giving speed of response; to be sufficiently flexible and well-trained to be able to adapt quickly to rapidly evolving operational environments; and to be ready to deploy and operate worldwide, most likely with our key allies and partners.

DELIVERING THE FUTURE

We have outstanding platforms and capabilities that will allow us to do all of this, but we must develop further our understanding and ability to integrate those capabilities and gain maximum effect, especially in the information environment; and to fuse air, space and cyber capabilities within fast, agile, multi-domain command and control. This is an enormous challenge, but I know we will succeed. It will require constant change and transformation in the way we think and operate – but then the willingness and ability to innovate, adapt and improve has always been an essential part of the RAF story. And we continue to have outstanding people in the RAF, across every branch and trade – their extraordinary skills, motivation and commitment are what will deliver the Next Generation Air Force and secure our future.

In our 100th anniversary year, we cherish the rich heritage of the RAF. Our history has shown us that we need to be ready – today, tomorrow and every day – to meet the challenges that will confront us in the air, in space and in cyber. We have done so with enormous success throughout our first 100 years and we can be confident that we will continue to do so in the future, as we head with immense pride into our second century.

A DISPLAY OF AIR POWER

A century of RAF history is exhibited in central London and around the country as part of the RAF100 celebrations. By Ms Zerrin Lovett and Warrant Officer Simon Hardwick

In 1946, as part of the Royal Air Force's contribution to the postwar Victory Parade, it placed aircraft in Green Park for the public to see. The parade, which took place on 8 June, itself had an impressive flypast of 300 aircraft.

The RAF continued to display aircraft in the centre of London to commemorate the Battle of Britain throughout the 1940s and 1950s, with one of the last taking place on 11 September 1960. The aircraft in that exhibition have mainly survived, with XM479 Jet Provost still flying, in a private capacity. The last significant exhibition on Horse Guards Parade took place between 8 and 15 September 1968 to commemorate the 50th anniversary of the Royal Air Force. The aircraft from 1968 then became part of the initial collection of the newly formed RAF Museum.

The exhibition at Horse Guards of nine aircraft, both historic and contemporary, which will be open to the public from 6 to 9 July, aims to recreate the ethos of the past while showcasing the air force of today. The RAF has been incredibly fortunate that so many museums, along with BAE Systems and Lockheed Martin, have offered to loan their historic and facsimile aircraft, so that they can offer a great insight into the service's rich and diverse history. Veterans, re-enactors and serving aircrew will be with the aircraft to tell the stories of who flew these wonderful flying machines.

The aircraft will provide a backdrop to the 10 July celebrations, where a reception will be held for up to 5,000 serving and retired RAF personnel and special guests on Horse Guards Parade Square. A touring display of aircraft is taking place throughout 2018, visiting Cardiff, Newcastle (Northern Ireland), Birmingham, Glasgow and Manchester.

KEY EXHIBITION DETAILS

- The Aircraft Tour will be in London on Horse Guards Parade and open to the public from 6 to 9 July, from 11am to 6pm

- No tickets are required for the public sessions, but the event site will be cordoned off and visitors will enter through a queuing system and security check

- The access point will be from Horse Guards Road (by St James's Park), at the north-west corner

- From 9am to 11am each day group visits (schools, youth organisations, veterans, etc.) will have pre-planned access to the Horse Guards Parade Tour area

- There will be a fast-track lane for group and VIP visits and this can also be used by people with Ministry of Defence ID cards (MOD civil servants, contractors and all service personnel)

- It is strongly recommended that, to facilitate access, people do not bring bags

- Dogs (other than assistance dogs) will not be permitted

- There will be nine aircraft on display – a mix of heritage, operational and facsimile models, tracing the centenary of the RAF. They will be: BE2C, Spitfire MkXVI, Dakota C4, Meteor F4, Harrier GR3, Tornado GR4, Chinook, Typhoon and Lightning II

- There will be information boards and personnel at each aircraft to engage with visitors

- There will also be a STEM (science, technology, engineering and maths) Zone with activities and RAF100 merchandise and souvenir programmes for sale.

"The exhibition aims to recreate the ethos of the past while showcasing the air force of today"

Opposite (clockwise from the top left): A Hawker Tempest, Gloster Meteor, Hawker Hunter and English Electric Lightning at the RAF Battle of Britain Display, September 1968

Right: A Supermarine S6b seaplane at the same exhibition on Horse Guards Parade

AIRCRAFT OF THE EXHIBITION

ROYAL AIRCRAFT FACTORY BE2C

(replica on loan from the Allied Air Forces Memorial and Yorkshire Air Museum)

The versatile BE2C, built by the Royal Aircraft Factory in Farnborough, was one of the most widely used British aircraft of the First World War. It served in all three services and heralds the Royal Air Force's genesis in the Royal Naval Air Service and the Royal Flying Corps. Although it had great stability, it was vulnerable to attack by more manoeuvrable German monoplane fighters during the "Fokker Scourge" of 1915–16 and the "Bloody April" of 1917. Fighter versions serving with Home Defence Squadrons flew by night and, despite lacking any additional equipment to assist them, shot down five raiding German airships over the UK in 1916.

This particular aircraft is loaned from the Allied Air Forces Memorial and Yorkshire Air Museum and is a replica 1914 aircraft built by RAF Halton engineering apprentices. It was used by the Royal Air Force as a display aircraft for many years. Its fantastic display condition is testament to the hard work of volunteers in the Yorkshire Air Museum's Heritage Engineering team with help from apprentices from all over Europe.

Dimensions: Span 36 ft 10 in/11.23 m; length: 27 ft 3 in/8.30 m

Date: 1914–18

Use: Two-seat reconnaissance, bombing, artillery spotting, training and home defence (as a single-seater)

Engine: 70 hp Renault WB/WC or 90 hp RAF 1a inline engine

Top speed: (RAF 1A engine) 72 mph/116 km/h

Maximum altitude: Service ceiling 10,000 ft/3,050 m

Armament: The first armed variant of the BE2, with a Lewis machine gun in the observer's front cockpit, severely limiting its field of fire. Bomb load of 224 lb/102 kg below belly

Where used: Northern and southern Europe, Middle East, Egypt, East Africa, North Africa, India

SUPERMARINE SPITFIRE MKXVI

(on loan from the RAF Museum)

The Spitfire, originally designed by RJ Mitchell, went on to be probably the most recognisable aircraft of the Second World War. It was developed as a single-seat day fighter and used by the RAF and other allied forces. It went through many re-designs, with this Spitfire XVI being the last variant with a Merlin engine. The Spitfire XVI was built as a low-altitude fighter, with a specially optimised engine and clipped wings. Later production aircraft, like this example, featured a cut-down rear fuselage and bubble canopy.

This particular Spitfire, on loan from the RAF Museum, was flown as the personal aircraft of the Air Officer Commanding Fighter Command Air Marshal Sir William Elliot with 31 Squadron (Metropolitan Communications Flight) at RAF Hendon from July 1950 until October 1953. A replica Spitfire has just been mounted as a gate guardian at the Museum in the markings of a London squadron – 601 "Millionaires" Squadron, so called as it was formed from a group of aristocratic and very "well-heeled" young men, most of whom could have afforded to have their own aircraft and had previously been amateur pilots.

Dimensions: Wing span 32 ft 7 in (clipped wing)/9.75 m; length: 31 ft 4 in/9.6 m

Date: 1944–57

Use: Single-seat day fighter/fighter-bomber

Engine: 1,720 hp Packard Merlin 266

Top speed: 405 mph at 22,000 ft/650 km/h at 6,700 m

Maximum altitude: Service ceiling 42,500 ft/12,954 m

Armament: Two 20 mm cannon and four 0.303 in machine guns, mounted in wings. Could carry 500 lb/227 kg of bombs underwing or underbelly

Where used: UK, Northern Europe, Germany

GLOSTER METEOR F4

(on loan from the RAF Museum – usually on display at the Tangmere Military Aviation Museum)

The jet age is represented by a British and RAF first – the Gloster Meteor F4, the first British jet fighter and the Allies' only jet aircraft to achieve combat operations during the Second World War. Its development was heavily reliant on its groundbreaking turbojet engines, pioneered by Sir Frank Whittle. The Meteor F Mk 4 was the first postwar variant of the Meteor, developed in 1945. It equipped 22 squadrons of Fighter Command and was widely exported. In May 1950, it was the first jet fighter to be based in Scotland.

In September 1946, Group Captain EM "Teddy" Donaldson DSO, AFC of the RAF High Speed Flight flew a modified version of the Meteor F Mk 4 from RAF Tangmere and achieved a world airspeed record of 615.78 mph at Rustington off the Sussex coast. This particular Meteor, on loan from the RAF Museum, is Group Captain Donaldson's record-breaking aircraft.

Dimensions: Span 37 ft 2 in/11.32 m; length: 27 ft 3 in/8.30 m

Date: 1945–56

Use: Single-seat interceptor fighter

Engine: Two 3,500 lb Thrust Rolls-Royce Derwent 5 turbojets

Top speed: 585 mph/941.46 km/h at sea level

Maximum altitude: Service ceiling 44,500 ft/13,563 m

Armament: Four 20 mm Hispano cannon in nose

Where used: UK

DOUGLAS DAKOTA C-47B

(on loan from 16 Air Assault Brigade Association)

The Douglas C-47 Dakota is probably the most celebrated transport aircraft ever built. It was developed from the DC-3 commercial airliner and remains in worldwide service even today. During the Second World War, Dakotas served in every battle zone and were the mainstay of both the RAF and the US Army Air Forces transport squadrons. The design was so popular it was widely copied by other air forces, including those of Russia and Japan.

This particular Dakota was built in 1946 and served with the RAF as KP208 in India. It last flew on 18 May 1970. 16 Air Assault Brigade, an organisation with strong ties to the RAF, has loaned KG374 from its gate guardian position at Merville Barracks, Colchester Garrison. KG374 was the last to have served with the RAF and is still playing her part in its proud history today. She is joined on Horse Guards by veterans of all UK Armed Forces who took part in Operation Plainfare – the British contribution to the Berlin Airlift of 1948–49. This response to the Soviet blockade of West Berlin is still the longest and largest humanitarian aid airlift in history. The Royal Air Force continues its global humanitarian aid and disaster relief operations around the world today.

Dimensions: Span 95 ft/28.96 m; length 64 ft 6 in/19.65 m

Date: RAF 1943–70 (and BBMF 1993–today)

Use: Passenger/freight transport and glider towing

Engine: Two 1,200 hp Pratt & Whitney Twin Wasp R-1830-92 radials

Top speed: 230 mph/370 km/h

Maximum altitude: 23,200 ft/6,960 m

Armament: Normally none carried, but some in India carried two Browning machine guns in door or windows for defence against Japanese fighters

Where used: (RAF) Northern and Southern Europe, North Africa, Middle East and Far East, West Africa, North America, Germany, Palestine, Egypt, India, Burma, Malaya, Singapore, Hong Kong, Australia

HAWKER SIDDELEY HARRIER GR3

(on loan from the RAF Museum)

The Harrier was another world first for the Royal Air Force and British engineering excellence. The world's first operational VSTOL (vertical short take-off and landing) aircraft, it entered the Royal Air Force just after its 50th anniversary and served for over 40 years in all theatres of operation. The Harrier GR3 was developed from the Harrier GR1 in 1972, but with the addition of a laser target marker housed in an extended nose section. The GR3 is renowned for its role in the Falklands Conflict of 1982.

This particular aircraft, XZ997, has been loaned for the display by the RAF Museum and has a rich history. Commissioned in the late 1970s, she initially served in Germany before serving in the Falklands Conflict of 1982. XZ997 operated in a ground attack and reconnaissance role with 1 Squadron from the carrier HMS *Hermes*, covering the British landings at San Carlos Water and also attacking Port Stanley airfield. It was also flown by the late Air Chief Marshal Sir Peter Ted Squire, GCB, DFC, AFC, DL, FRAeS.

Dimensions: 25 ft 3 in/7.70 m; length 46 ft 10 in /14.27 m

Date: 1972–94

Use: Single-seat, tactical ground attack/fighter

Engine: 70 hp Renault WB/WC or 90 hp RAF 1a inline engine

Top speed: 738 mph/1,191 km/h

Maximum altitude: Service ceiling 51,200 ft/15,605 m

Armament: Two 30 mm ADEN cannon in underbelly pods, 5,300 lb/2,385 kg of stores on four underwing and one underbelly pylon, including SNEB rocket packs. Some modified to carry two Sidewinder AAM

Where used: UK, Germany, Belize, Falkland Islands

TORNADO GR4

(on loan from the Royal Air Force)

The Panavia Tornado, developed jointly by the UK, West Germany and Italy, was designed for high-speed, low-level attack missions. This example of pan-European cooperation resulted in a fantastically successful aircraft. Its truly multi-role capabilities meant that it replaced several different fleets of aircraft in the air forces that it served when it was commissioned in the late 1970s and will continue to serve in the RAF until at least 2019.

The Tornado GR1 and GR1A were both capable of carrying a large number of bombs and missiles. They flew during the First Gulf War, in 1991, attacking Iraqi airfields and using laser-guided bombs against bridges, fuel depots and weapon dumps. The model on display at Horse Guards is the GR1B variant, developed to carry the Sea Eagle missile while retaining the GR1s avionics and weapons capability. This aircraft will go from Horse Guards to serve proudly as the gate guardian at RAF Lossiemouth in Scotland.

Dimensions: Span (fully extended) 13.9 m/45 ft 7 in; span (wings fully swept) 8.6 m/28 ft 2 in; length 16.7 m/54 ft 10 in

Date: 1980–2001

Use: Two-seat all-weather tactical strike aircraft

Engine: Two 16,920 lb thrust Turbo-Union RB199 turbofans

Top speed: 1,490 mph at 3,000 ft/2,400 km/h at 914 m

Maximum altitude: 15,240 m/50,000 ft

Armament: Two 27 mm Mauser cannons 8,165 kg (18,000 lb) load including: eight 454 kg (1,000 lb) bombs, two JP233 airfield denial weapon, two Paveway laser-guided bombs, two Sidewinder air-to-air missiles. In the Maritime Strike Role: Two Sea Eagle anti-ship missiles

Where used: UK, Germany, Middle East, Balkans

BOEING CHINOOK HC MK 4/6

(on loan from RAF Odiham)

The Chinook aircraft represents the proud rotary aviation history of the Royal Air Force that began in 1945. It provides all branches of the British Armed Forces with heavy-lift support and transport, and has been used extensively in combat, humanitarian aid and disaster-relief operations at home and abroad. Its use as a flying emergency room has saved many lives and is supported by serving and reserve medical personnel, highlighting advances in aviation and battlefield medicine over the RAF's 100-year history.

Popularly known as the "Wokka-Wokka", due to the distinctive noise of its tandem blades in flight, the Chinook workhorse has been a faithful RAF servant since 1980, having been in United States service since 1962. In total, 72 were delivered to the Royal Air Force, of which 60 remain in service in three variants. The glass-cockpit-equipped HC Mk 4 fleet is currently being upgraded to the same standard as later-delivered HC Mk 6 aircraft.

The Chinook on display here is ZA718/BN "Bravo November", on loan from RAF Odiham. This well-known 1982 Falklands Campaign veteran continues in frontline service; four of its pilots have earned the Distinguished Flying Cross (DFC).

Dimensions: Rotor diameter (each) 60 ft/18.29 m; length 51 ft/15.54 m

Date: 1980 (original HC Mk 1)–today

Use: Heavy-lift support helicopter for trooping for up to 55 troops, resupply with up to 10 tonnes of mixed cargo and battlefield casualty evacuation. Crew of four – two pilots and two crewmen – plus role specialists as required. Much used for emergency response in UK such as helping in rebuilding flood defences damaged by winter storms

Engines: Two 4, 168shp Honeywell T55-714A turboshaft engines

Top speed: 184 mph/296 km/h

Service ceiling: 15,000 ft/4,572 m

Armament: Two 7.62 mm M134 miniguns mounted in cabin windows and one 7.62 mm M60D machine gun mounted on rear ramp for hostile fire suppression

Where used: Based at RAF Odiham, Hants and RAF Benson with 7, 18, 27, and 28 Squadrons, Chinook Display Team and RAF Falcons Parachute Display Team. Also Germany, Afghanistan, Balkans, Iraq, Sierra Leone, Falkland Islands

BAE SYSTEMS EUROFIGHTER TYPHOON FGR4, 2008

(full-scale facsimile on loan from BAE Systems)

The Eurofighter Typhoon is the most advanced multi-role combat aircraft available on the market today and continues the European collaborative defence cooperation of the earlier Tornado. In this case, the Typhoon is a product of a partnership between the UK, Germany, Italy and Spain. It was initially employed in an air-to-air fighter role.

The current upgraded Typhoon FGR4 is an extremely agile multi-role combat aircraft. Although the Typhoon's primary role is for air defence, it has been deployed in a wide range of air operations. It conducts 24/7 year-round protection of the UK's sovereign airspace on quick reaction alert, and is regularly deployed on air policing, peace support and high-intensity missions around the world. It has also been used against Da'esh targets in Syria and Iraq. The aircraft on display at Horse Guards is a full-scale replica of the FGR4.

Dimensions: Span 35.9 ft/10.95 m; length 52.4 ft/15.97 m

Date: 2008–today

Use: Single-seat multi-role combat aircraft and two-seat advanced trainer

Engines: Two Eurojet EJ200 turbojets, each with 20,000 lb thrust

Top speed: 2.0 Mach (1,521 mph)

Maximum altitude: 55,000 ft/16,764 m

Armament: Enhanced Paveway II and Paveway IV guided bombs, AMRAAM and ASRAAM missile, one Mauser 27 mm cannon. Future weapons will include the Meteor air-to-air, and Storm Shadow and Brimstone air-to-surface missiles

Where used: UK, Northern Europe (Arctic, Baltic and Black Sea regions), Falkland Islands, India, North America, Libya, Syria, Far East

LOCKHEED MARTIN UK F35/ LIGHTNING II, FROM 2018

(full-scale facsimile on loan from Lockheed Martin)

Lockheed Martin's F-35 has been in development since 1997 and is the result of a partnership between over 1,500 companies from nine countries. There are three variants now in use by 12 nations. Each has slightly different capabilities. The "A" variant takes off and lands conventionally; the "B" variant is designed for short take-off and vertical landing (STOVL); and the "C" variant is designed to fly from aircraft carriers. The F-35B Lightning fifth-generation combat aircraft will operate alongside the RAF Typhoon and is a multi-role machine capable of conducting air-to-surface, electronic warfare, intelligence gathering and air-to-air missions simultaneously.

The aircraft combines advanced sensors and mission systems with low-observable technology, or "stealth", which enables it to operate undetected in hostile airspace. Its integrated sensors, sensor fusion and data linking provide the pilot with unprecedented situational awareness. The pilot can share information gathered by the jet with other platforms using secure data links, and/or use the information to employ weapons or electronic means. The F-35B's short take-off and vertical landing capability allows it to operate from the new Queen Elizabeth-class aircraft carriers and the vessels of allied nations, as well as short airstrips.

Dimensions: Span 35 ft/10.7 m, length 51.2 ft/15.6 m

Date: 2018

Use: Multi-Role Fighter/ground attack/reconnaissance aircraft

Engine: 40,000 lb thrust Pratt & Whitney F-135-600 turbofan

Top speed: Mach 1.6 (1,200 mph)

Maximum altitude: 50,000 ft/15,240 m

Armament: Carries Paveway IV bombs and AMRAAM and ASRAAM missiles

Where used: USA (trials and training), UK

FORGING INSPIRATION

A newly commissioned trophy celebrates the RAF100's themes of past, present and future

Traditionally, the Royal Air Force marks its anniversaries by commissioning a piece of silverware. These pieces form part of the RAF's rich history and are often displayed in messes or station headquarters, where they provide a continuing connection with the past for those serving. Each piece of silverware is either donated or paid for through contributions from messes or associations.

When the RAF decided to mark its centenary in 2018 with such a piece, it was faced with the small problem of how to fund it. Air Marshal Sir Ian Macfadyen stepped up with a suggestion that he find a benefactor to assist with the costs. He introduced Melissa John (a businesswoman, philanthropist and collector of RAF gallantry medals) and Stephen Connelly (Director of Cleave, Court Jewellers and Medallists) to the Chief of the Air Staff, Sir Stephen Hillier. Melissa generously offered to donate a suitable piece of silverware to the RAF in memory of her brother, the aviation historian Christopher John.

RAF100 has three themes: commemorate, celebrate and inspire. Sir Stephen decided that he wanted to use the commissioned piece of silverware as a trophy for a new annual award to be introduced in 2018. Individuals and teams around the RAF are being nominated, so that it can be presented during the celebrations on 10 July.

Cleave suggested four designs and Sir Stephen chose a unique one incorporating two aero trails. The initial design did not include any additional elements, but Sir Stephen suggested that perhaps the Spitfire and Lightning II could be placed at the top of each of the two silver trails. This sterling-silver centrepiece conveys flight with images of two iconic aircraft reaching up to the skies, moving through the air, with sterling silver aero trails spiralling down and continuing over the base.

The magnificent blue enamel base represents both the RAF and the skies, and is patterned with overlaid silver gilt strips to symbolise and continue the aero trails theme, suggesting speed and movement. The current crest of the Royal Air Force is applied to the front of the enamelled base, with the King's crest on the reverse to represent the formation of the RAF in 1918.

The base of the trophy is inscribed as follows:

The RAF Centenary Trophy
Presented by Melissa John
In memory of her brother,
aviation historian
Christopher John

The RAF Centenary Trophy for Inspiration represents 100 years of innovation, design and technological advancement, qualities of which the RAF is proud and that it will continue to maintain over the next century.

THE RAF100
FLYPAST

One of the most thrilling highlights of the centenary celebrations will
be the RAF100 Flypast, which takes place over The Mall in London on 10 July.
This is the result of months of painstaking preparation, planning and coordination,
and comprises an array of aircraft from throughout the RAF's 100-year history.

Referred to collectively as the "Windsor Formation", each of the Flypast's
20 sections will fly under a different callsign, from "Vortex" to "Red Arrows",
as profiled over the following pages.

Flying in style 51	Blackcat 66
Maintaining the force 55	Snapshot 67
	Tartan 68
Vortex 58	Goose 69
Spectre 59	Sentry 70
Dakota & Memorial 60	Aggressor 71
Warboys 61	Ninja 72
Swift 62	Monster 73
Snake 63	Gibson 74
Zorro 64	Typhoon 75
Grizzly 65	Red Arrows 76

FLYING IN STYLE

The RAF100 Flypast represents one of the biggest in RAF history and will celebrate the service's illustrious centenary on a grand scale

The flypast of "Windsor Formation" on the 10 July 2018 draws together all three goals of the Royal Air Force in its 100th year – to commemorate, celebrate and inspire. The composition and size of the Flypast is truly momentous and worthy of the celebration of the centenary of the world's first independent air force. It is comprised of virtually every platform that the RAF currently operates, but to safely and efficiently generate such a spectacle, an incredible amount of planning has been completed over the previous 12 months.

The Flypast's Project Officer is Wing Commander Kevin Gatland, Chief of Staff at the Tornado GR4 Force Headquarters operating from RAF Marham. Wing Commander Gatland has been responsible for all elements of the coordination of the project, drawing operational and instructional experience as a Tornado GR4 Navigator to pull together all of the necessary components, both military and civilian. Before detailed planning could commence, engagement

across the RAF was required to ascertain feasibility on the size, duration and formations of the Flypast, which aircraft types and squadrons would participate, and the final order of aircraft.

This extraordinary number of aircraft – over four times as large as the annual Queen's Birthday Flypast – required detailed liaison and integration with the Civil Aviation Authority to ensure that huge areas of busy and congested UK airspace were safely de-conflicted, while retaining maximum civilian usage and flexibility to continue operating into the national, regional and minor aerodromes in the south of England. Significantly, the cooperation of London Heathrow, London City Airport and numerous civilian airfields was critical to formulating a workable "concept of operations" for the Flypast. All of this liaison had to be documented and approved and set out in an "Operation Order" and distributed to all involved from the RAF's Chief of the Air Staff down to the most

"The RAF100 Flypast epitomises the ethos of the RAF, with every role combining to create a spectacle that will commemorate, celebrate and inspire"

junior of rank working in air traffic control or an operations room, as well as a myriad of civilian organisations.

Once the concept of operations of the Flypast had been agreed, Wing Commander Gatland along with Squadron Leader Matt Axcell and Squadron Leader Mo Abdallah commenced the task of detailed "tactical-level" planning of individual aircraft and formation routes. Squadron Leader Axcell and Squadron Leader Abdallah, of 31 Squadron, who operate the Tornado GR4 from RAF Marham were also assigned the prestigious callsign of "Windsor Lead" on 10 July 2018. Hosting numerous meetings, the team worked following the concept of a safe "chock-to-chock plan", with the crew painstakingly and meticulously specifying every individual aircraft's route and timings from the first turn of a propeller or turbine to "wheels stop" on landing. The plan was constantly iterated as new information was obtained from both the squadrons involved, as well as the expert guidance of the RAF air traffic control team.

SMART COMMUNICATIONS

Led by Squadron Leader Lorraine Hawthorne and Warrant Officer Mel Young, a robust communications plan was required. This incorporated the RAF and civilian controllers of RAF(U)

Opposite: RAF100 Flypast Leaders Squadron Leader Matt Axcell (left) and Squadron Leader Mo Abdallah

Swanwick, located at National Air Traffic Services, as well as RAF and civilian controllers at airfields across the United Kingdom. The controllers were responsible for the safe and expeditious passage of the aircraft flying over London on 10 July but also played a crucial role in bringing over a hundred aircraft together as one formation in East Anglia before safely dispersing and routing them back to their home airfields across the UK.

The planning process culminated with two days of intricate formation planning held at RAF High Wycombe and RAF Marham, where all of the individual formation lead aircrew were brought together and the aircraft routes finalised prior to the release of the Flypast Operation Order. Prior to these planning days, additional sites were selected to have elements of the Flypast overfly. These included the northerly runway at Heathrow Airport, the RAF Memorial at Runnymede, Windsor Castle and the RAF Museum at Hendon. Each of these locations required comprehensive planning and coordination. The planning phase was concluded on 28 June when the team presented the Chief of the Air Staff and Air Vice Marshal Gerry Mayhew, the Senior Responsible Officer for the Flypast, with one of the most complicated and detailed UK multi-formation plans ever devised. With their approval, the task of turning the ambitious plan into airborne reality began.

During June, individual aircraft types had been rehearsing their specific formations and manoeuvres, with the immense task of generating such large numbers of aircraft calling upon the skill and expertise of the individual squadron engineers and aircrew. This was all completed while still maintaining operations across the globe, protecting UK skies and generating training output for our future generations of pilots, aircrews and engineers. The superlative work of the engineers was matched by every trade across the RAF, with logistics, operations, administration and communications being fully involved in generating the largest single mass of aircraft seen for many decades.

Prior to the main event on 10 July, approval and a final confirmation of the Flypast was required by the Senior Responsible Officer for the Flypast, Air Officer Commanding, No.1 Group, Air Vice Marshal Gerry Mayhew. This requirement was satisfied by a successful practice flypast conducted over RAF Cranwell, which served as a fine stand-in for Buckingham Palace and saw the aircraft flying the intricate plan to split-second timing. With a host of senior RAF officers and VIPs observing from the ground, the final approval for the historic Flypast was granted.

And so to 10 July 2018, exactly 100 years and 100 days after the formation of the world's first independent air force. The RAF100 Flypast epitomises the ethos of the RAF, with every single trade and role combining to create a spectacle that will commemorate our glorious past, celebrate our current achievements and inspire future generations throughout the second century of Her Majesty's Royal Air Force.

10 FASCINATING FLYPAST FACTS

The facts and figures behind the RAF100 Flypast really bring home the magnitude of this magnificent celebration

1 The Flypast is the most formidable mass of Air Power ever assembled by the RAF, consisting of cutting-edge technology and highly trained aircrew, capable of completing missions across the breadth of defence output.

2 The Flypast consists of 100 aircraft of 23 types, with nearly 200 aircrew from 25 different squadrons, operating from 14 RAF stations and three civilian airfields. Over the course of the Flypast, Air Traffic Control will communicate with the aircraft on more than 50 unique radio frequencies.

3 The Flypast planning has taken nearly a year, with countless working hours, thousands of emails and phone calls, dozens of small planning meetings, two "force element" planning days, one mass brief, numerous individual formation rehearsals and a full rehearsal flypast – itself requiring a fully detailed bespoke plan!

4 When all 100 of the Flypast aircraft converge over Buckingham Palace, they will be within 15 km of each other.

5 Safety is the prime concern and for the Flypast to go ahead on 10 July the weather must meet exacting criteria even though some aircraft, such as the Tornado GR4, are quite capable of flying in cloud at 200 ft and 600 mph, safely avoiding obstacles and the ground by using its terrain-following radar.

6 The Hercules celebrates its 52nd birthday this year.

7 The formation also contains brand new aircraft with the H135 Juno, H145 Jupiter, 120TP Prefect and F-35B Lightning all entering active service within the timescale of the formation planning.

8 The lightest aircraft is the 120TP Prefect at a maximum take-off weight of 1,440 kg. The heaviest is the C17 at 265,350 kg, 185 times heavier!

9 The largest aircraft is the Voyager. It is the largest that the RAF has ever operated, with a length of 58.82 metres and a wingspan of 60.30 metres.

10 The FGR4 Typhoon is the fastest aircraft in the Flypast at Mach 1.8; the slowest are the helicopters, although the RAF's new F-35B Lightning can also hover and even go backwards.

MAINTAINING THE FORCE

Whether for operations, exercise, training or a centenary flypast over The Mall, the safety aspects of each Royal Air Force flight are always the same, and always crucial

The shout comes through from the operations desk. "Crews walking in 10 minutes!" Adrenaline kicks in.

Aircraft service books are made ready for the aircrew to check and sign. The maintenance teams that have been working through the night, servicing and repairing the jets from their previous flight have completed their work and made them ready for the next sortie, ready for the aircrew to fly.

The line team are dispatched to the aircraft handling area to prepare the airframes that are sat in the morning haze for their next flight. The engineering hit team is assembled: airframe riggers, avionics fairies, engine mechs, armourers and safety equipment specialists. It takes a whole team to get the aircraft airborne. The specialist engineering kit is ready: crypto, blanks and pins removed. One of the aircraft has a problem on start-up. The engineering team make their way to the jet and troubleshoot. Every see-off

can be a challenge. Complacency has no place here. Professionalism is everything.

"On the early morning see-offs when they light the afterburners you can feel the vibrations in your chest as they depart for another sortie," says Senior Aircraftman Callan Griffin, an aircraft maintenance mechanic with 31 Squadron, Operation SHADER 2018. "It's the teamwork bit I like."

DIFFERENT EVERY TIME

The operations desk calls again. "Ten minutes out!" The aircraft will be returning shortly. Every time, and under every condition, the scenario presented is different. Regardless of the weather or environment, the job needs to be done. Taxi in; stop; tyre check; roll over; brakes. As the turbines slowly wind down, the engineering team swarm the aircraft to prepare her for her next sortie.

"We are 100 years away in terms of technology but the feeling is still the same when these aircraft climb into the air – job well done"

Opposite: RAF technicians work on a Chinook helicopter during a pre-deployment exercise

Right: Flight Lieutenant John Mercer

"Fuel! Oil! Oxygen! No snags, Sir? Reload the weapons?" The story goes on. Away from the flight line, the off-duty engineers seek to recharge weary bodies and tired minds through the camaraderie of the bar, pushing weights in the gym or relaxing across the station.

"The young men and women who make up the line teams are worthy successors to the same breed who held down the wings of those early bi-planes as they taxied across the desert before clawing their way into the air over dusty foreign lands," says Warrant Officer Butterfill from 31 Squadron, who fly the Tornado GR4. "We are, quite literally, 100 years away in terms of technology but the feeling is still the same when these aircraft climb into the air – job well done by the ground crew, facilitating the completion of the mission by the aircrew."

FAMILY OF FLIGHT

The engineers work in close proximity to the same aircraft every day and night and they, like the aircrews, become like an extended family. You know how to coax a particular aircraft through a pre-flight built-in-test even when it's trying its best to thwart you. You know how to set out the seat straps on the next morning's aircraft to allow for an easier crew-in. You know that one engine tends to be a bit thirsty on the oil. But once every system is up and running and the engines accelerate the aircraft down the runway, the professionalism and expertise of the engineering team will allow the crews to complete their tasks in an often lonely and inhospitable environment miles above the ground. It is this accomplishment and teamwork that makes engineering in the RAF so much more than just a job.

"The role of an engineer in the modern-day RAF is to carry out high-precision technical tasks on our state-of-the-art, next-generation equipment to the highest possible standard every single time," says Flight Lieutenant John Mercer, RAF Engineering Officer. "It's about giving the brave men and women in the cockpit the right tools and equipment they need to do their jobs at home and abroad as safely as possible."

VORTEX

The RAF Support Helicopter (SH) Force operates for the Joint Helicopter Command and includes the Chinook (based at RAF Odiham) and the Puma (based at the RAF Benson). Both stations provide critical, rapid support for UK military operations throughout the world and deliver direct support to the Field Army, Royal Marines and UK Special Forces. They can be tasked in a variety of roles including assault trooping, transport, refuelling and aeromedical evacuation. Both SH platforms are incredibly versatile and are able to operate in all weathers, day and night and in any environment.

The Puma helicopter is based at RAF Benson with 33 and 230 Squadrons and is currently supporting the on-going NATO training mission in Afghanistan. The small footprint of the Puma makes it ideal for landing in urban areas. Two Pumas can fit into a C-17 Globemaster and be delivered anywhere in the world, where they will be ready to fly again just four hours after being unloaded. This proved invaluable when hurricanes hit the Caribbean in 2017, with the Puma arriving in between hurricanes to deliver vital emergency aid to stricken communities.

RAF Odiham has three Chinook squadrons: 7 Squadron, 18 (Bomber) Squadron and 27 Squadron, with the latter providing heavy lift. They provide UK national standby at very short-notice readiness, as well as supporting current operations worldwide, and were also deployed to the Caribbean last year both on land and with the Royal Navy from HMS *Ocean*. Most recently they deployed to Cumbria during snowstorms to deliver much-needed fuel and food to communities isolated by heavy snowfall.

Both types are supported by a joint Operational Conversion unit, 28 (Army Co-operation) Squadron, and Joint Helicopter Support Squadron based at RAF Benson.

Above: 27 Squadron Chinook crew Flt Lt Jenny Boyd, Sqn Ldr Jay Berry, FS Pete Welsh and Sgt Kelly Fitzpatrick

SPECTRE

The Defence Helicopter Flying School (DHFS) provides helicopter training for pilots and rearcrew from the Royal Navy, Royal Marines, British Army and Royal Air Force, as well as partner nations. It takes them to a level where they are ready to move on to operational aircraft with frontline conversion units. It achieves this output by starting all students on a core programme of flying training before individual services move on to advanced courses within the school, tailored to the requirements of their future operational roles.

The school now operates the H135 Juno as the primary training aircraft, as well as three H145 Jupiter aircraft at RAF Valley. These new aircraft represent a leap in technology compared to previous types and provide an excellent platform to prepare students for the rigours of operating increasingly complex frontline types in the most challenging of environments.

Students of all services progress through basic training on 2 Maritime Air Wing (MAW), comprising 660 Squadron Army Air Corps (AAC) and 705 Naval Air Squadron, before progressing on to advanced courses with 9 Regiment AAC, comprising 670 Squadron AAC and 60 Squadron, RAF. Mountain and maritime modules are also completed with 202 Squadron at RAF Valley. Students graduate from the DHFS ready to train on their frontline aircraft types and continue the Tri-Service, multi-role interoperability that they have built throughout their training.

Command of the DHFS sits with the Station Commander of RAF Shawbury. The Senior Operator is an RAF Wing Commander, Commanding Officer 2 MAW is a Royal Navy Commander and Commanding Officer 9 Regt AAC is a Lieutenant Colonel. The mix of all services gives the students invaluable experience and prepares them for a future of joint operations. Ascent is the training provider company, which parallels the military with its leadership structure, including a team of senior aircrew instructors and ground training staff.

Below: Flt Lt Blake, Sqn Ldr McDowell (Ac Capt) and Sgt Duncan

Below: Battle of Britain Memorial Flight, RAF Coningsby

DAKOTA & MEMORIAL

The RAF's Battle of Britain Memorial Flight (BBMF) epitomises the commemorative element of the RAF100 celebrations, remembering all those who have lost their lives serving in the Royal Air Force, or its predecessor the Royal Flying Corps, in all conflicts from 1914 up to the present day. In most cases those who made the ultimate sacrifice were volunteers who willingly signed up to the risks. Perhaps all that they would ask in return is an understanding of what they did, of the hardships and trials they faced, and to be remembered. The RAF BBMF fleet of Second World War aircraft is preserved in flying condition as a living tribute to them. The flight's motto "Lest We Forget" says it all.

As one might expect, the BBMF has been inundated with requests for flypasts, filming and photography to support RAF100 projects. It was heavily involved in filming for the *RAF at 100* documentary shown on the BBC in March and the www.starrship.space website that features one of the RAF's Spitfires.

Meanwhile, the BBMF carries on with its day job of maintaining and displaying its unique fleet. Many thousands of people all across the UK get to see the aircraft flying, while in its hangar the BBMF enables World War Two veterans from the UK and the Commonwealth to get close to aircraft of the types they once flew in or maintained. And everybody, young and old, can come in via its Visitor Centre in Coningsby, Lincoln.

WARBOYS

The RAF centenary year is an exciting time for Elementary Flying Training (EFT) as it transitions to a new aircraft and new way of training. EFT is spread over four squadrons – at RAF Cranwell (57 Squadron), Barkston Heath (674 Army Air Corps Squadron and 703 Naval Air Squadron) and Wittering (16 Squadron). Part of No.3 Flying Training School, the EFT's job is to teach pilots from the RAF, the British Army and the Royal Navy how to fly.

The Grob Tutor has been the mainstay of EFT since the millennium and has trained all of defence's pilots since then. In 2018, the RAF replaced the Tutor with the Grob Prefect, a significantly more capable aircraft that will much better prepare RAF pilots for the Next Generation Air Force. With well over twice the power, a digital glass cockpit and a retractable undercarriage, the Prefect is a step change. It is run in partnership with Ascent, the RAF's new Military Flying Training System, which brings improved infrastructure, courseware, IT and – for the first time for EFT – simulators to train the students.

The three Prefects on the RAF100 Flypast come from 57 Squadron at RAF Cranwell. Led by Wing Commander Ian Bews, Officer Commanding EFT, they represent the first stage of flying training for new pilots and are one of the newest aircraft in the RAF's inventory.

Above: Flt Lt Mike Foran, Wg Cdr Ian Bews, OC Elementary Flying Training and Flt Lt Martin Killen

SWIFT

72 Squadron flies the Tucano T1 as a Basic Fast Jet Trainer at No.1 Flying Training School (FTS), RAF Linton-on-Ouse, training all RAF and Royal Navy Fast-Jet pilots. The Tucano has served the RAF for more than 25 years and goes out of service in October 2019, handing over to the new Texan T6 at RAF Valley, which will be a huge leap forward in technology. Students on Tucano learn to fly formation, advanced handling and navigate to find targets at low level, with only a map and stopwatch, before being awarded their Fast Jet Wings and progressing to the Hawk T2.

The squadron's instructors represent the whole RAF with fast-jet, helicopter and multi-engine pilots, bringing a range of experience to its students. It also relies on a "Whole Force" of support: Babcock, its contract partner, maintains its aircraft, and the squadron is directly supported by civil servants and a few of its instructors are reservists.

72 Squadron celebrated its own centenary in the summer of 2017, and No.1 FTS, the oldest flying training school in the world, celebrates its centenary next year. The squadron has a long history including the Battle of Britain, the early jet age and almost four decades of helicopter flying, before reforming in 2002 into its current role. The squadron's crest bears the motto "Swift", so the call-sign for its "diamond nine" formation was easy to pick. It is proud to be part of the RAF100 Flypast and hopes to use it as an example of its mission: "To train tomorrow's fast-jet pilots today."

Below: A Tucano training flight passing Scarborogh

"Participating in the Flypast celebrating the 100th anniversary of the RAF is a great honour for us"

SNAKE

The Shadow R1 is operated in the Intelligence, Surveillance and Reconnaissance (ISR) role by 14 Squadron based at RAF Waddington. The aircraft is a modified version of the civilian Beechcraft King Air 350 series and entered service in 2009 as part of an urgent requirement to support Operation Herrick in Afghanistan. Through its comprehensive suite of sensors, the aircraft is able to provide vital real-time information to commanders on the ground. Currently a fleet of five aircraft, the SDSR in 2015 approved a purchase of three additional aircraft and guaranteed support for the platform through to 2030. Currently in development in partnership with Raytheon systems, a comprehensive upgrade to R2 standard in the coming years will ensure the type remains at the forefront of the RAF's ISR capability through its service life.

Above: 14 Squadron Shadow R1 crew Flt Lt Paul Norton, Sqn Ldr Matt Leyman and Sqn Ldr Bird

The Shadow R1 is taking part in only its second public flypast over Buckingham Palace following last year's Queen's Birthday Flypast. The element lead for Snake formation is Squadron Leader Matt Leyman who joined the RAF in 2003, originally flying the C-17 Globemaster for five years before moving onto an instructional role teaching students and instructors on the Grob Tutor. "Participating in the Flypast celebrating the 100th year of the Royal Air Force is a great honour for us," says Leyman, "and we are delighted to be asked to take part." The Shadow force has been almost continually deployed on operations since its inception and remains so today.

ZORRO

Celebrating its 52nd birthday in the Royal Air Force this year, the C-130 Hercules is the longest-serving operational aircraft in current service. The C-130 has been continuously deployed at the forefront of global operations and will continue to do so into the future. At the end of the Falklands Conflict, over 36 years ago, it was the first British tactical transport aircraft to land at Port Stanley and the C-130 fleet maintained a presence at Mount Pleasant until April this year, before handing over to the A400M Atlas. The C-130 was also the first British aircraft to land in various conflicts: in Kuwait after the Iraqi retreat, in Bagram during the liberation of Afghanistan and in Tripoli during the withdrawal of UK civilians from Libya.

47 Squadron currently has two C-130s continuously deployed to RAF Akrotiri in Cyprus, where they act in support of Operation Shader in Iraq.

The C-130 and all squadrons who operate her are now based at RAF Brize Norton, having moved from RAF Lyneham in 2011. The crew flying in the RAF100 Flypast is made up of personnel from 47 Squadron, the operational frontline squadron; XXIV Squadron, the operational conversion unit; and 622 Squadron Royal Auxiliary Air Force, who provide aircrew and flying support personnel to the C-130. "It is an honour to take part in this historic event," says 47 Squadron's Commanding Officer, "particularly in an aircraft type that has been in service for more than half of the RAF's 100-year history and one that will remain at the forefront of tactical air mobility for many years to come."

Above: 47 Squadron aircrew members

*Below: Atlas C Mk1 crew Flt Lt
Dave Ellis, Flt Lt Gary Davidson
and MACR Ozzy Hicks*

GRIZZLY

The Atlas C Mk 1 is the latest multi-engine airlifter to join the RAF fleet. The first aircraft was delivered to RAF Brize Norton in November 2014 and the Atlas Force has steadily increased to the current 18 out of a planned 22 aircraft.

The Atlas is a marked step change in capability for a turbo-prop powered tactical airlifter. As well as normal airports it can operate from natural surface runways such as grass, sand or gravel. The maximum unrefuelled range is in excess of 6,000 km; the equivalent of flying from London to Chicago. As an airlifter it excels with a cavernous freight bay some 17 metres long by 4 metres square, which can take a maximum payload of 35 tonnes – three times more than a C-130J Hercules.

The aircraft is currently operated by XXIV, LXX and 206 Squadrons, with 30 Squadron resuming frontline operations later this year. XXIV Squadron is the operational conversion unit and trains all of the aircrew and engineers for the aircraft. LXX Squadron is currently the sole operational frontline squadron while 206 Squadron is the trials and development unit that clears new capabilities for the aircraft.

The Atlas has already proved its worth in RAF service supporting military operations around the world, with aircraft currently deployed to the Falkland Islands and the Middle East. The Atlas Force is on constant readiness and was rapidly deployed last year to provide much needed humanitarian aid to the Caribbean Islands devastated by Hurricane Irma.

BLACKCAT

The C-17 Globemaster III, operated by 99 Squadron at RAF Brize Norton, is the backbone of the Air Mobility Fleet. It provides the ability to transport vast quantities of vehicles, equipment and personnel to the furthest corners of the earth, 365 days a year and at short notice. The aircraft specialises in carrying outsized loads such as Chinook helicopters and heavily armoured vehicles to keep Britain's ground forces safe. The most powerful aircraft in the RAF, the C-17 can produce 161,600 lbs of thrust from its engines, which is needed because, fully laden, the C-17 weighs 585,000 lbs – the equivalent of 200 family cars or 2.5 blue whales!

In its 100th year, 99 Squadron continues to fly missions around the globe in support of national interests. Recently it has provided aeromedical evacuation to recover critically ill patients back to the UK and provided humanitarian relief, with the C-17 being the first RAF aircraft to deliver aid in the aftermath of Hurricane Irma in the Caribbean. The squadron is also supporting the United Nations by delivering vital medical supplies to South Sudan and supporting military operations in Iraq, Afghanistan and Syria.

99 Squadron has also recently celebrated its own centenary, where personnel honoured the history and tradition of the squadron while remembering the fallen with a royal parade. "This is a historic year for 99 Squadron that provides the opportunity to pay respect to the courage, determination and adaptability of all of those who have served on this prestigious unit," says Wing Commander Marc Holland, the Officer Commanding 99 Squadron. "As we look to the next 100 years, I am confident that future members of 99 Squadron will continue to live up to their motto, '*Quisque Tenax*' – Each One Tenacious."

"This provides the opportunity to pay respect to the courage of all those who have served on this prestigious unit"

Right: 99 Squadron flight deck crew and loadmaster

SNAPSHOT

V(AC) Squadron is extremely proud to be flying the Sentinel R1 in the RAF100 Flypast. Although more usually, Sentinel can be found flying at much higher altitudes, providing wide area surveillance of the ground. Put simply, in an era of fake news and reports that can be distorted by social media, the Sentinel's mission is to provide decision makers with the objective truth. Whether it is assessing the impact of flooding in Somerset, looking for the kidnapped Chibok schoolgirls in Nigeria or hunting Da'esh in the Middle East, the squadron is constantly in high demand. Even now as it celebrates the RAF's centenary, Sentinels are actively deployed on operations.

The Flypast crew are Tom, Chris, Dutch, Andrew, Mark and Daryl. They come from all over the UK and from a variety of backgrounds but their common dream was to join the RAF. Tom, for instance, was sponsored by the RAF through university – inspired to join from the age of four, when he first saw the Red Arrows at the Liverpool Airshow. Chris just couldn't wait and joined straight from school at 16, rising to the rank of Sergeant before commissioning as a pilot.

The whole team has been deployed on operations around the world. Between them they have conducted a wide variety of missions including strike, search and rescue, counter-terrorism, anti-drug smuggling, anti-submarine warfare and tactical airlift. From the Arctic to Antarctica, from Hawaii in the West to Singapore in the East, from underground bunkers to 50,000 ft in the sky – between them they have truly served across the globe.

Above: V(AC) Squadron Sentinal R1 crew Sqn Ldr Tom Blackwell (Captain), Flt Lt Mark Buxton, Flt Lt Andrew Dearing and Flt Lt Chris Edmondson

Below: Voyager crew Flt Lt Adam Mercieca, Sgt Andy Emberton and Flt Lt James Beattie

TARTAN

The RAF's Voyager aircraft is operated by 10 and 101 Squadrons in the Air Transport and Air-to-Air Refuelling Role. The Voyager entered service in 2011, replacing the RAF's fleet of VC10 and Tristar aircraft and immediately began support to RAF operations worldwide, including Afghanistan, Falkland Islands and more recently in Iraq and Syria.

For today's RAF100 Flypast, the Voyager is being crewed by Flight Lieutenant Adam Mercieca of 10 Squadron, Flight Lieutenant James Beattie of 101 Squadron and Sergeant Andrew Emberton, also of 10 Squadron. Flight Lieutenant Adam Merceica, 36, originally from Cardiff, joined the RAF in 2003 after studying astrophysics at Cardiff University. Posted to the VC10, Adam served on operations in Iraq, Afghanistan, Libya and the Falklands. After crewing the last VC10 sortie

as part of their farewell flypast, Adam was posted to Voyager in 2015.

Flight Lieutenant James Beattie, 33, originally from Huddersfield, joined the RAF in 2005. Posted originally to 216 Squadron flying the Tristar, he served on operations in Afghanistan, Libya and the Falklands. After flying the last operational sortie of the Tristar, Beattie was posted to 101 Squadron in May 2014.

Sergeant Andrew Emberton, 39, originally from Lincolnshire, joined the RAF in 2007 and began his career as a linguist, learning Pashto for 18 months. After crossing over trades to become an Air Loadmaster, Emberto served on the 216 Squadron Tristar until being posted to the Voyager as a Mission Systems Operator in 2014. The crew is looking forward to supporting the RAF100 Flypast immensely and is proud to be involved in such a historic event.

GOOSE

The RC-135 Rivet Joint is the aircraft element of the UK Airseeker project and is based at RAF Waddington, Lincolnshire. 51 Squadron is equipped with three Rivet Joint aircraft, which are employed to deliver battle-winning Signals Intelligence capability, supporting national and theatre requirements globally. The information the aircraft provides enables commanders to make informed decisions about the environment before them, from the strategic to the operational to the tactical level.

51 Squadron celebrated its centenary in May 2016 and has been employed on operations in the Middle East, Mediterranean and Europe since delivery of the first Rivet Joint aircraft in 2013. The Rivet Joint programme works closely with the USAF and the personnel of the 55th Wing at Offutt AFB in the USA. In a unique arrangement, RAF and USAF personnel can be employed on each other's aircraft under a co-manning agreement.

"The Rivet Joint is at the forefront of the UK's airborne signals intelligence capability," says Air Commodore Dean Andrew, ISTAR Force Commander. "It is being used to good effect on operations from Waddington and as required by defence."

Squadron personnel will be commemorating RAF100 with the ISTAR Force at RAF Waddington. They recently celebrated the RAF and USAF's shared heritage, in April, at a RAF100 and USAF 70 event in Omaha, Nebraska – the USAF base for Rivet Joint aircraft. The RAF100 Flypast aircraft will be captained by Officer Commanding 51 Squadron, Wing Commander Simon Cloke.

*Above: 51 Squadron flight
deck personnel*

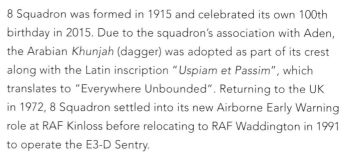

Left: Flt Lt Gemma Robertson,
E-3D Surveillance Operator

Below: Wg Cdr Jez Batt, Officer
Commanding 8 Squadron

SENTRY

8 Squadron was formed in 1915 and celebrated its own 100th birthday in 2015. Due to the squadron's association with Aden, the Arabian *Khunjah* (dagger) was adopted as part of its crest along with the Latin inscription "*Uspiam et Passim*", which translates to "Everywhere Unbounded". Returning to the UK in 1972, 8 Squadron settled into its new Airborne Early Warning role at RAF Kinloss before relocating to RAF Waddington in 1991 to operate the E3-D Sentry.

In addition to supporting national RAF100 events, 8 Squadron have been celebrating the 100th anniversary with a dinner dance and a charity bike ride. The squadron has also supported RAF100 celebrations overseas by flying an E-3D Sentry and crew over to NATO Airbase Geilenkirchen in Germany to support RAF personnel serving overseas. The squadron will gather and raise a glass to celebrate this very important year, sharing stories of the many deployments and the operations 8 Squadron has been involved in. The charity bike ride will be an incredible endurance challenge where four members of 8 Squadron will cycle the entire 874 miles from Land's End to John O'Groats raising money for four separate charities including the RAF Benevolent Fund and the RAF Association.

In July, the squadron will complete its participation in the RAF100 celebrations with its inclusion in the mass flypast over London, while other members of the squadron parade the colour on The Mall. "I am extremely proud of 8 Squadron's inclusion in the RAF100 Flypast," says Wing Commander Jez Batt, Officer Commanding 8 Squadron. "It is a once-in-a-career opportunity for us to partake in such a prestigious event and it is a fitting addition to the squadron's already rich history."

*Below: 100 Squadron Hawk T1 crews Flt Lt
Moncrieff, Maj Hudson (USAF), Sqn Ldr Arlett,
Flt Lt Peters, Flt Lt McCann and Sqn Ldr Taylor*

AGGRESSOR

100 Squadron, operating out of RAF Leeming in North Yorkshire, now forms the RAF's only Red Air Aggressor Squadron. With an illustrious background spanning more than 101 years and 18 aircraft, 100 Squadron – or "the ton" as the squadron is sometimes better known – has operated some of the RAF's finest aircraft for more than a century. These include the FE2B in the First World War, the Lancaster bomber in the Second World War, through to the Canberra, the Victor and currently the Hawk T1.

Easily identifiable by its skull-and-crossbones crest, 100 Squadron was last seen over London during the Diamond Jubilee flypast where it led the iconic "E II R" formation. The squadron has proven its potency over the past century, with a crucial and broad role today. It truly lives up to its squadron motto: "*Serang Tebuan Jangan Dijolok*", which translates as "Never Stir up a Hornets Nest". The motto is in Malay in recognition of the squadron's activity in what is now Malaysia during the Second World War, and due to the fact that it was based in Malaya during the Malayan Emergency.

NINJA

IV Squadron aims to deliver world-class fighter pilots to the front line using the innovative Hawk T2 aircraft. Using cutting-edge datalink technology, it emulates the Typhoon cockpit and sensors, while simultaneously providing a "computer game" simulation of a modern 3D battlefield.

While flying this modern, agile jet trainer, the next generation of fighter pilots are tested with air-to-air and ground-to-air threats that develop their cognitive decision-making skills and teach them the tactics, techniques and procedures they will need to thrive on the front line. Experienced and talented Qualified Flying Instructors and support staff, based at RAF Valley in North Wales, provide operational know-how from around the world and delivery outstanding flying training.

Students are taught initially how to fly and operate a fast jet at up to 500 knots and 42,000 ft before quickly moving to tactical serials requiring basic fighter manoeuvres and attack profiles. Later on, they move to 2v1 Beyond Visual Range (BVR) engagements using simulated radars, missiles and electronic warfare and countermeasures, day, night and in cloud. Finally, they learn how to operate safely and effectively as single-seat operators on a self-escort mission using profiles that Typhoon and F35 could use on operations. The course is one of the most demanding in the world and graduates of IV Squadron will be well placed to help secure the skies in the next century of military aviation.

Below: A IV Squadron Hawk T2 formation approaching RAF Valley

MONSTER

Weapons checked, crew strapped in. Mission data loaded, pre-flight checks complete. Throttles to maximum power, Rolls-Royce engines winding up. The roar; afterburners lit; we're off. Another pair of Tornado GR4s charge along the runway and take to the skies to complete their mission.

The Tornado has been at the centre of the RAF's strike capability for almost 40 years and has evolved into today's dynamic platform that can deliver effects precisely where and when they are needed. Striking multiple targets from long range, collecting reconnaissance imagery, supporting troops from directly overhead with live video feed of their enemy's position and accurate weapons; the Tornado has proven itself time and time again.

"I feel the same excitement today as I crew into the Tornado that I felt when seeing them fly over my head at low level through the Glens of Scotland as a kid," says Flight Lieutenant Steve Smith, a pilot with 31 Squadron. "I feel incredibly lucky to have been part of the Tornado's story and my heart still races today when I see her with wings swept, thundering through the sky."

The men and women that have flown, maintained and supported the Tornado during its prestigious career have all played their part and have a story to tell. The "mighty fin", as she is affectionately known, will retire soon but will continue doing what she does best right to the end. Having been on continuous operations for 27 years, 2019 will mark the end of an era and will bring a tear to many an eye, but the Tornado's legacy will live on. RAF personnel will take their experience and knowledge onto future aircraft and ensure the lessons learnt during Tornado's momentous career are not forgotten.

Right: Tornado GR4 crew
Flt Lt Steve Smith, Pilot and
Sqn Ldr Mo Abdallah, WSO

GIBSON

"It is apt that the most potent air asset the UK has ever possessed, the F-35B Lightning, has arrived home at RAF Marham"

RAF100 is an especially significant event for 617 "Dambusters" Squadron, having reformed in the RAF's centennial year. The RAF has been at the forefront of cutting-edge technology in the defence of the nation since its conception, and it is apt that – as the RAF celebrates its 100th anniversary – the most potent air asset the UK has ever possessed, the F-35B Lightning, has arrived home at RAF Marham.

2018 also marks 617 Squadron's 75th anniversary. Formed in 1943 as a specialist flying unit, and initially tasked to attack the dams of the Ruhr industrial area, the squadron went on to be involved with many more special operations throughout the war, and indeed throughout the past 75 years.

This historical precedent provides a unique focus for all members of the squadron and is the bedrock of 617's ethos to this day. Throughout the RAF100 celebrations, the Royal Air Force and Royal Navy personnel serving on 617 Squadron will be taking the opportunity to pause and reflect on the past 100 years of technical innovation, while also looking forward to bringing F-35B Lightning into frontline operational service towards the end of the year. This is a game-changing capability for the squadron, the RAF, the RN and wider UK defence, and in keeping with the legacy of the men and women of 617 Squadron and the Royal Air Force before them.

Above: The F-35 Lightning arrives at RAF Marham

TYPHOON

The Typhoon Force contribution to the RAF100 Flypast is very much a collaborative effort, with aircraft coming from RAF Coningsby, Lincolnshire and RAF Lossiemouth, Moray. Personnel from all five frontline squadrons and the Operational Conversion Unit will be involved in the Flypast. In fact, this will be the largest formation flypast that the Typhoon Force has ever conducted and is a fitting celebration of the RAF's 100th anniversary. For the Flypast, the aircraft will all operate from RAF Coningsby and it will take just under eight minutes to get all 22 aircraft airborne.

The Officer Commanding 29 Squadron has the auspicious task of leading the formation on the day. "I am immensely proud to have been selected to lead the Typhoon formation," he says, "and it will be the culmination of many months of meticulous planning and preparation."

One of the other formation pilots will also be marking a significant achievement, having flown in a Hawk T Mk 1 for the 75th anniversary of the RAF and taking part in the centenary celebrations. "To be able to take part in two significant milestones in the history of the RAF is a real privilege," he says.

Warrant Officer Jon Hooper, 29 Squadron, is leading the engineering plan for the Flypast and will be coordinating the 390 engineers who will be preparing the aircraft. "It is a real logistical puzzle that requires careful planning to achieve success," he says.

Right, bottom: Wg Cdr Andy Chisholm, Officer Commanding 29(R) Squadron

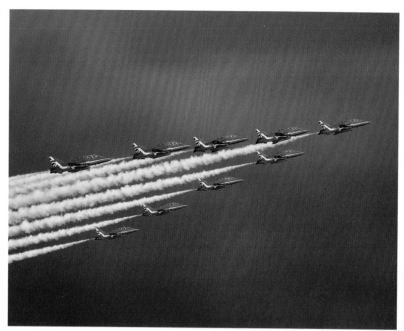

RED ARROWS

In 2018, the Royal Air Force Aerobatic Team, the Red Arrows, is performing to millions of people at more than 60 events, as part of the service's centenary year and the squadron's 54th display season. Based at RAF Scampton, Lincolnshire, the Red Arrows first displayed in 1965. Since then they have performed almost 4,500 times in 57 countries – promoting the best of British and supporting UK industry, which is another key role of the team.

The squadron is commanded by Wing Commander Andrew Keith and the nine-aircraft formation led by Red 1, Squadron Leader Martin Pert. The team flies BAE Systems Hawk T1 fast-jets and comprises 130 personnel, including pilots, engineers and essential support staff with frontline experience. Together, they inspire people with a display of precision and teamwork in the air and on the ground. These aerobatic shows and colourful flypasts showcase the

agility of the RAF, aid recruitment to the Armed Forces and help to represent the UK at home and overseas.

As well as displays and flypasts, the team is marking the RAF100 year by participating in several ground-based activities, with many highlighting the importance of the STEM subjects of science, technology, engineering and maths.

"It is particularly special, in 2018, to be a member of the Red Arrows, as we celebrate the RAF's centennial year," says Wing Commander Andrew Keith. "It is a chance to reflect and consider achievements and lessons learned from the past 100 years and to look forward with energy and vision to the next chapter of the RAF's evolution. It is a privilege to command an exceptional group of people that fly the flag for the UK and we are grateful for the overwhelming public support we receive each year."

Above, right: Wg Cdr Andrew Keith, Officer Commanding, Royal Air Force Aerobatic Team

ACKNOWLEDGEMENTS

By Zerrin Lovett, RAF100 Chief Operating Officer

RAF100 has been an exciting programme to deliver and it has been a team effort. I would like to thank the following people for working so hard on RAF100. There are so many people to say thank you to and below are just a few of those to whom we owe a massive debt.

PROGRAMME TEAM

The Air Force Executive Board and Air Officers' Commanding 1, 2, 22 and 38 Groups and the Regional Air Officers for Scotland, Wales and Northern Ireland

Air Vice-Marshals Knighton and Wigston

Air Commodores Barrow and Toriati

Group Captains Sanger-Davies, Radcliffe, Walcot

Wing Commander Andy Kime for being the only part-timer who works over 60 hours a week

Wing Commander Sonia King

Squadron Leader Jo Roe – for helping me put the whole programme together

Squadron Leader Becky Frame

Flight Lieutenants Alex Ball and Mike Bennett

Warrant Officer Simon Hardwick, who volunteered for three months and stayed for two years

All our various holding officers – you know who you are!

PROJECT OFFICERS

RAF100 has been really lucky to have so many individuals who've helped out and gone above and beyond to make our events and initiatives a success:

Wing Commanders Glynis Dean and Russ Barnes for embracing the challenge of creating a massive educational programme

Group Captain Ange Baker and Squadron Leader Ruth Fordyce for managing the Horse Guards event

Group Captain Rob Wood and Squadron Leader Daniela Nowalski, who bravely took on the Baton Relay and made it a brilliant 100-day event

Wing Commander Paul Crook, Squadron Leader Barry Matthews and the Ceremonial Office for being amazing to work with and creating the best PowerPoint presentation that I've ever seen

Wing Commanders Morgan and Taylor, Flight Lieutenant Dougal Gow and Master Aircrew Master Whelan for help with the Aircraft Tour

Squadron Leader Tom Benson, for being great fun to work with and delivering some amazing events

Wing Commander Kevin Gatland and Flight Lieutenants Nosh Chaudry, Jonathan Eddison and Rebecca Causer-Smith

Wing Commander Tara Scott, Squadron Leaders Albie Smith and Nobby Clark from the regional offices

Rich Fogden and Wing Commander Neil Hope for sports and football.

OTHERS

We have been fortunate enough to receive so much more help than we'd normally expect from across the RAF. A few people deserve a special mention:

Steve Watts and all the other Director of Resources staff who've embraced the challenges that we've thrown at them

The Air Staff for helping when things got fraught

Media and Communications, especially Group Captain Nick Bayley and Wing Commander Odette Hardcastle from Directorate of Defence Communications

Our many STEM Champions without whose efforts we wouldn't have inspired so many children

The RAF100 Appeal charities and volunteers.

RAF100 APPEAL SPONSORS

The Royal Air Force and the four major Royal Air Force charities are most grateful to the following RAF100 Appeal sponsors for their support

HEADLINE SPONSORS

SPONSORS

RAF100 APPEAL

As we celebrate the centenary of the Royal Air Force in 2018, commemorating with pride those who have served and are serving today, we must continue to inspire those who might serve their country in the future, as those in the past have done

In order to Inspire and Support the next 100 years, the Royal Air Force and the four main RAF charities are combining together in this unique opportunity to help and assist the entire RAF family. The RAF100 Appeal will focus on ensuring that all members – past, present and future, are honoured, supported and inspired. Your help is needed to support tens of thousands of individuals – from the youngest child to the oldest veteran, and thus leave a lasting legacy for years to come.

WHO WILL BENEFIT FROM THE RAF100 APPEAL?

YOUNG PEOPLE

- Through the development of engaging programmes in engineering and expanding the coverage of our aerospace STEM subjects
- By enhancing the range of scholarships and university bursaries available for those wishing to enter the professional world of aviation and aerospace – particularly focussing on attracting those from under-privileged backgrounds
- By providing a range of 21st Century aerospace training facilities and equipment
- Through the improvement of children's education and the provision of a safe and secure environment, playparks and childcare centres
- By providing a social network through youth clubs for RAF children of all ages to make friends with others experiencing similar challenges
- By significantly increasing the number of flying experiences and training opportunities.

SERVING PERSONNEL

- Through the provision of the very best support, advice and relationship counselling for those families in most need as well as those in financial distress
- By helping families to remain strong, communicate better and by providing facilities for children to visit separated parents
- Through the development of facilities to ensure our servicemen and women can build their skills for the future and receive respite from the rigours of operations.

VETERANS

- By improving independent living through housing and garden adaptations and the provision of mobility equipment
- By ensuring that any veteran in need of help is given the very best standard of support and counselling
- Through the introduction of new initiatives to combat loneliness and social isolation
- By providing respite facilities and domiciliary care to allow veterans to live their twilight years with the dignity and respect they deserve.

These are just some of the priority projects that your support for the RAF100 Appeal will make possible. If you would like to help, or find out more information about how you can support the appeal, please contact: Sophie Gomez Sarabia Tel: 020 7307 3301 E-mail: sophie.gomez-sarabia@rafbf.org.uk

The RAF100 Appeal is a joint venture between the Royal Air Force, Royal Air Forces Association, the Royal Air Force Benevolent Fund, the Royal Air Force Charitable Trust and the Royal Air Force Museum. Funds raised will be divided between the four participating charities and charitable projects nominated by the Royal Air Force in support of the RAF family.
www.raf100appeal.org

PUBLISHER
St James's House
298 Regents Park Road
London N3 2SZ
Phone: +44 (0)20 8371 4000
publishing@stjamess.org
www.stjamess.org

Richard Freed, Chief Executive
richard.freed@stjamess.org

Stephen van der Merwe, Managing Director
stephen.vdm@stjamess.org

Richard Golbourne, Sales Director
r.golbourne@stjamess.org

Ben Duffy, Communications Director
ben.duffy@stjamess.org

Stephen Mitchell, Head of Editorial
stephen.mitchell@stjamess.org

Aniela Gil, Senior Designer
aniela.gil@stjamess.org

John Lewis, Deputy Editor
john.lewis@stjamess.org

Picture credits
UK MoD Crown Copyright, Getty Images,
Sgt Paul Oldfield, PA, Squadron Prints, RAF
Museum Collection, Charles Brown Collection

St James's House, Regal Press Limited
298 Regents Park Road, London N3 2SZ

www.stjamess.org

Printed by CPi Colour on Chorus Silk.
This paper has been independently certified
according to the standards of the Forest
Stewardship Council® (FSC)®.

A catalogue record for this publication
is available from the British Library.

ISBN: 978-1-906670-57-3

All information in this book is verified to
the best of the authors' and publisher's ability.
However, Regal Press Limited does not accept
responsibility for any loss arising from reliance
on it. Where opinion is expressed, it is that of
the author or profiled organisation and does
not necessarily coincide with the editorial views
of the publisher. The publishers have made all
reasonable efforts to trace the copyright owners
of the images reproduced herein, and to provide
an appropriate acknowledgement in the book.

The inclusion of sponsor organisations in this
publication does not constitute an endorsement,
implied or otherwise, by the publisher or the
Royal Air Force. Any readers wishing to use the
services of these organisations should take up
independent references in the normal manner.

The publisher would like to thank the following:
328 Support Services GmbH
AW Hainsworth
Alzheimer's Society
Arnold Clark Automobiles
Aviva Plc
AWE
Baines Simmons Ltd
Bank America Merrill Lynch
BMT
Bristol Airport
Bristow Group
Byron College, Greece
Caribbean Aviation Training Center
CCM Motorcycles
Cobham PLC
Defence Discount Service
East of England Ambulance
  Service NHS Trust
Edinburgh Napier University
Estelon
Ex-Mil Recruitment
Frequentis
Gatwick Airport
Government of Gibraltar
Grenson
Greyfriars Vineyard
Hamilton
Hampshire County Council
Hawk Yachts
Heathrow Airport
Hornby Hobbies
Hornsey School for Girls
Iberia Maintenance

IBM
JuMelia Ltd
Kent, Surrey & Sussex Air Ambulance Trust
KP Training & Consulting Ltd
Leighton Academy
London City Airport
London South Bank University
Mark Physsas Architects
Martin Kemp Design
Meggitt PLC
Ocean Software
Pearson
PrivateFly
Rimowa
Sharon Khazzam
Shropshire Council
Signature Flight Support
Skyworld Aviation
Sodexo
Spitfire Heritage Gin
Surrey County Council
TAG Aviation
The Alice Smith School, Kuala Lumpur
The Black Farmer
The Cheadle and Marple Sixth Form College
The Institute of Leadership
  and Management
The London Boroughs
The Poppy Factory
The Shed Inc.
Ultra Electronics
University of Derby
Vantage Aviation
Visit Malta